Mountain

An Evolutionary Epic

Jeannie —
Thank you so much for
your encouragement and
support. I hope the
book engages and inspires
you in your ongoing path
through earth and cosmos

— Bill

Mountain

An Evolutionary Epic

William Carney

PAN/GAIA BOOKS

ISBN 978-0-9886944-0-8

PAN/GAIA BOOKS
San Rafael, California

Design template, Julie Valin, The Word Boutique
Cover design, Anthony Puttee, BookCoverCafe.com
Editorial & design advice, Mark Livingston

Printed in the United States

Other poetry by William Carney:

Cities, a nuclear peace poem
Beaches, an environment of poems
Sunflower Futures
Pacific Slope

You may browse, purchase and comment at
www.williamcarney.net

In memory of

Sam Ciofalo,

mountain man

Contents

.6. Friday

.7. Saturday

Preface

During my lifetime, our species has delved its deep sources in space and time with growing accuracy. We now hold a common creation story that reaches forth from the first instant of existence to our own precious 'moment in the sun,' wherein we marvel that we are in fact descendants of light, constituted of stardust and still nursing on the radiance of a star. It's a creation story capable of spanning all others, bridging stubborn human differences and beginning to heal our long, painful and ultimately illusory separation from planet and cosmos, and perhaps even from one another. This is the story that *Mountain* sings.

Our wide-eyed wonder at this new awareness has found its temple in the earth itself, and its icon in a simple, space-born photograph of our one azure home, singularly emergent from the dark expanse of the universe.

During my lifetime, our species also has steadily desecrated this temple. We've recklessly extracted and exploited the planet's 'resources,' reshaping material reality to fit human wants that we also intentionally refashion into ever more whimsical and rapacious hungers. We've heedlessly spread our populations, wastes and toxins throughout the world, endangering both ourselves and the integral systems that support all life. We've shredded the sacred texts of planetary experience scripted in the genes of the innumerable species that we have driven to extinction, unread and often unknown. We have threatened creation with weapons of instantaneous oblivion, casually bantered.

And now our unthinking combustion of fossil carbon has triggered changes to the earth's climate and oceans that will forever alter the planet's 'way of life,' intensifying the impacts of all our other derelictions.

During my lifetime—lived within what we hold to be an exemplary democracy—our species has collectively chosen *not to see* what it is doing, not to recognize its place in creation as a conscious and responsible power and to act accordingly. By demagogues and dollars, we've led ourselves astray. We've intentionally looked away. We've chosen to be blind. But also in this lifetime, we have felt from time to time the awareness of the entire planet come alive and transfigure in a single moment—looking back at the borderless earth from space or watching the threadbare truths of the cold war dissolve onto the rich compost heap of history.

We inhabit such a moment of seismic insight and heroic challenge. Our worldview is shifting—and with it, the world we live in and create each day. Perception is that sharp a tool. Vision is that powerful a motivator.

The hopefulness of the poem is rooted in this moment and in three imperatives it plainly presents us: to know our place on earth and in the universe, to act responsibly based on that knowledge, and above all *to see clearly*. Or more precisely, in the spirit of both art and science, to see clearly over and over again—to actively allow an ever iterative clarity to evolve and to inform our actions. For our cosmic creation story is also the story of our own creativity, and both remain unfinished and unfathomable.

How you might approach this poem

The poem pursues these basic themes through a
simple story of young backpackers in the high
Sierra wilderness. For a week, each evening
around the campfire they listen to the story of the
universe unfold, and they share in 'songs' the
stories of their own unfolding lives. It's all
written down in June's journal. Here's a
typographic Rosetta Stone for following these
multiple voices:

> The body of the poem, the campfire
> **universe story** told by Dave the naturalist, is
> set in 'Garamond' type, like this preface.
>
> The **individual songs** of Jose, Lily, June, Mo,
> Vince, Marta, Gwen and Meru are set in this
> 'Optima' typeface (*italicized when they
> speak as a group*).
>
> *Finally, this 'Baskerville Old Face' oblique font
> marks the personal notes and entries of the
> journal keeper, June. It also carries June's voice
> through her duets with Mo and in her brief
> observations laced through Dave's narrative.*

This is, of course, a big story and a big poem, but
one arranged to be inviting. You may read it as
presented, day by day, tracking the various voices
and motifs as they interweave, resonate and
develop. Or you may wish first to focus
separately on the big-picture cosmic 'fire'
episodes, or on the sparks of individual 'songs'
(read in their nightly groupings or followed
character-by-character), or on June's individual
quest and questionings—and then consider how
these diverse strands interconnect.

Alternatively, as with any wild environment, you may find yourself simply wandering through the book, guided by unexpected prompts and impulses, stopping frequently to rest and ponder seemingly random details—while bearing in mind the overall terrain, inter-related ecology, and possible destinations. Whatever your preferred approach, guideposts through the chronology of the universe appear in the book's margins to assist your orientation. These are indexed in a 'Storyline of Cosmic Evolution' at the end of the text, together with a 'Storyline of June's Week' and a 'Key to Characters and Songs.'

But who is the *audience,* for whom is the poem written? Anyone, really. The story of the universe is the story of each of us. That said, the reader I invoked and imagined while writing the poem is a student, leisurely swinging on a front porch on a hot afternoon, as I once did, wending through a final summer reading assignment before returning to school or some other focused pursuit. So I would wish the poem to be a summer syllabus, background reading for the long work ahead.

Now, maps at hand, and with some sense of the topography and scenes to come, enjoy your ascent. And be aware, page by page, of the unfolding of your own life and consciousness in context with the evolution of the universe: how remarkable it is that the whole cosmos is this moment moving forward through your individual presence here within it, reflecting back its presence within you.

Mountain

1

.

Day One

Ascent

Circling up mountain as a hawk
might, on extended wing steadying
each turn, take on thin air—each stone here
each step up, impediment & lift
to higher ground, each sound sure-footed
as pinion on wind. Mind
      burdened as if
packing rock up mountain without end,
impacted thought, prescripted toxin.
Damn him. Damn
     trigger-happy dipstick
what he is. Hard heart he gives. Then wants
us back again as if nothing
means anything. Whole trip infected
with gross negligence. Whole mountain crushed
loose aggregate. What love was here once held
all things together. Now uncertain,
only me
    forever. Path, though, still
snakes on, the twelve of us all morning
winding up till sun dead overhead,
the mountain measured foot by foot, each
heavy breath cut short, incised as stone
(we want to think
      with some significance).
Heft stone above uncertainty, build
high. Lay stone foundation down. On sand,
on air, on emptiness. Who am I

here, reshaping self each step the shape
of earth?

       Rich cock-sure, crock-full, of answers,
everything that we must be. Life just
proceeds—spelled out, prix fixe, concrete.
Just stick to the routine (said genes
'conservative' by nature). Soon as
he finishes
        law school and me
            pre-med
we're 'set,' we'll 'knot' ourselves up good (pre-
packaged family man, 'responsible'
his brand) for service, pilot prep
for politics (the sky's the limit)
hurtling through stratosphere—
           eyes angle
down for balance here, crop up to catch
this instant this immensity (as Stein
said 'It's Picasso's world' first time she
flew, planed fields of Normandy fragmented
as stained glass below)—
        then maybe kid
& settling into respective
practices. Momentum
      holds one whole.

Have faith in that. The way my body
every step believes in gravity
and thereby in
      this rounding earth.
From birth, I think, I've felt this way.
Imagine that. Imagine
      back. Earth
tidal to all embryos, first pull
to orient first sphere of zygote,
then first neurons held in her liquid
massage, then globe of eye first thrilling
to red dawn of sunlight filtering

2

warm shallows, finally to join
long descent, head first, to dive into
full light and all encompassing round
world around which mind now fitfully
takes form.

            Belief enough, I'm thinking
how the planet spins me out, each day along
each path, umbilical.
                  Could I do that—
spin life from me, rotund as some domed
temple centering sun-drenched & cypress-
studded
            landscape? I'm wandering.
Doug fir the steeples here, Sierra
granite rising into air. Think thighs
the strength of mountains, calves turned taut
& sinewed with each scene. I am
geology the same and surely as
these peaks I now ascend.

                  Dad loves the plan,
daughter of his to carry forward
family lines. First girl to get this far. Check
that off (his backpack checklists late last
night, his endless preparations). Last step
for me to formally declare my
major and intents:
                  Two questions no
one's quested yet.
                  The answers here just
air, fire, water, earth—simplicity—life
then reconstitutes, stirs up towards
consciousness, likewise forever stitching
back together all creation. Walk
this path this brief duration.
                        Whole life
seems like
            I'm carrying—everything

now on my back. *(One false step, pack*
every which way teetering its queasy
lodestones pulling me
                              astray to plummet
down core empty shaft.) Stomach, too, too
stuffed—don't know what that's about—just want
to say to all of it 'get out, get
off.' (Me, too, I'm talking to.) No more
Rich 'will do right by me' whatever
happens. (That's Plan B. 'Big Bang directive'
Dad would say.) But I'm not buying it
now on, no way, no more. Eclipsed I am
high noon, all phases
                              off, all bets. What

if, what if, what if it iffing comes
to this—no choices left—laid down one
roll of tumbling mathematics in
clichéic hay? Meaning, I must now
find & thread
                              lost needle back to task
encompassing fields green of grain
& sensuous wave, flag-like
                              at mast-tip
as proud prow rides forward through up-
surging seas. So enter, sing in me
deep mystery. So surge inside to guide.

First fire: *We are here*

Dave
First say who you are and why you're here.

Vince
'To be outside. Not always locked in.'

Marta
'I sculpt. I'm opening. To granite.'

Gwen
'To exercise, like, every part of me.'

Meru
'Me 2, aka, build memory.'

Lily
'Just free me up from city's load of hurt.'

Jose
'To help with healing not done yet.'

Mo
'Face facts. Go quiet. Hear earth out.'

June
'*I'm June,' I say. 'I'm here to find my way.*'

Dave
And I'm a naturalist, just loving this
terrain of song—and all that walk it.

*Long silence brooding back on fires thought
long gone—then rising like frog chorus:*

All
'Tell us. A story. Teach us. The stars.'

You must first lose all other stories.
Lose yourself. Or what you have been told
you were. Only then you'll clearly see:
You are the stars. Teach me.

                              Caringly
he stirs warm embers, raising galaxies
into the air. He lays another
log.

          Watch this.

                    Long time he waits.

                              The fire
washes off the wood. Let it wash you
smooth as seashell or madrone, smooth as
manzanita on these hills. Fit thought
to wood, let fire polish down your words,
fit mind to it. Then you may begin
to see as fire sees. As stars see.
Open out
          your mind to be in

perfect state of possibility.
Think state
                    of grace, all things aflow in
unison as fire dances in caress
of wind, each medium transforming
mutual touch to something never felt
before, yet older than these flickering
mountains that embrace us.

                    Be open
to such touch, be moved by flex and flux
of stone (its mica insights), rush of
river spraying spectrums, or sudden
spark as cloud rolls loudly over peaks.

Let all things speak their lucid pentecost
in us, all tongues like fire here rise up.

Thoreau says *Simplify.* You need that here
just to survive. Hone down yourself
to what fits best, then carry it long
days as light as song. Try this to start:

We're all arisen from the earth, and earth
from stars, and stars from single burst
of energy from which all time & space
still radiates. No more. No less. That pulse
still travels through your heart, still speaks
in every breath magnificence in
you expressed.

Look inward as into
still pool—empty calm mind of surfaces,
be rid of boundary, deeply
reflect stars shimmering within. Your
eyes give back into the universe
its knowledge of itself, aswim &
glittering, deep well of time, wide ocean
brimming light we've gathered round tonight
to warm and reconnect. Our stories
rise, brief sparks rekindling the skies.

June's Song
(altitude)

So now
           they're saying
take it
           easy, rest, adjust

to altitude, breathe in
the thin

sky deeply—as if
so much
           clarity
takes
time

to reassemble, each
breath reassembling

                        me.

I'm entering
           arrangements
with a tree
           to keep me
clear &

           adequately
structured, heart
tethered

to earth, rooted

in air.

Rules of the Road
(we all agree)

Do not disturb
the anima.

Take only light,
leave only opera.

Pay attention,
everything is free.

No fires outside rings,
but burn within.

No sweets in tents—
intensely dream.

Know whereabouts
of friends.

Lose yourself,
find your song.

Let all things sing
respectfully.

Put back exactly
what you see.

Make room, make waves,
make way always.

2

. .

Monday

Second fire: *Earth*

So we begin. To see the stars look
down into the mica flecked within
this granite. All that
                    far grainy night
out there rests here in solid stone you
walk on every day. Take stone
                         in hand
& feel—in quartz, in feldspar—entire
crystal texture of the universe
here
            to be touched. The earth is starlight
come among us. Stars rained down &
gathered up to form all things. Stars streaming
to become us.

Star generations

              This granite's headstone
to a star. Your family ancestry
spans back through several. First
                              lit up half-
billion years from birth of universe.
All dying & reborn nine billion
years—long
                lineage of light. Each burns
through its inheritance of hydrogen.
(First
           shortage of first energy.) Then
fuses from it on hard anvil of

13.3 BYA - *stars
form from
hydrogen*

its own internalizing weight
more complicated elements. Spinning
together more & more
                    electrons
round centrific nuclei to blaze
increasingly
               intense. Till iron
that can't combust
                 collapses star in
final sacrificial flash gone
supernova (*super new*)—that instant
energized enough to cook all
other elements. Then
                strew them out
into
       prolific space.

13.2 BYA - stars & supernovae start forming other elements

Gravity takes hold

                 Desirous fire—
all colors, all directions licking—
orange, green, violet. Resolve myself
now back to prime. Be Mondrian
contained. Straight-lined.

                See glint of such
event. See supernova blink again
in granite. Touch
              stars exploding in
profusion. Their sharp shards. You hold now
in your hands. Feel
              weight of elements
stars generate. And earth still pulls down
hard into itself to make
              (as sculptor
might) of stone all things now known.
                    Then our
far-flung imaginings.
             So touch of
gravity takes hold and molds far drift

of stardust. First

to nebulae aswirl

with birthing new stars seeded

rich

with complex

elements. Fingers of which
toy inward round long vectors finding
equilibrium of orbit.
Over

time

snowballing self (dust
to dust repeatedly) to stone.

Then

planetoid. Till strength

of its own

gravity self-sculpts

round

earth.

Hard reckonings

Eons
on and on hard surface gets hard pounded
on. More

missiles coming in as

mounting mass more mass

attracts. Till throbbing

at its heart (pressed in by weight of self
as self accumulates) young planet
melts. And iron

(again) at heavy end

of mix pulls inward. Forming

liquid

core

internalizing

star-like

bulking

up enough to keep heat churning (stoked
by nuclear decompositions

12

also). Slowly in
        circuitous
convection grinding up cool rock of
crust
      to sink. Titanic
          into Vulcan
seas continuously alive from skies
astreak with
        boulders gravity's still
vacuuming from planet's path. Iron wand
also (slow circling) conjures
magnetic
      field to planetary shield
shunting aside rough rooting solar
winds.
      So silken atmosphere may purse
as yet unminted coin of earth.

          Think back
core moment in your own conglomerate
life still formative when
         some hard knock
or stress repeatedly (or even
love) smacks in
       & melts down everything
absorbed so far. Rendering every
experience back into liquid
state of possibility. Heart-felt.
From which
      life rounds itself & smoothes out
new amalgam orbiting
       one point
of light. In spirals ever twirling
through dark-sheened
      star-brimming space. In such
raw molten state
      earth's hit by hugest
sister planetoid down-splashing out

molten

moon

4.53 BYA –
moon forms
to pirouette. Its orbit
close enough to rip stone tides across
still dancing surfaces.

Temple & mausoleum

Bombardment
winding down through time crust cools.

New moon

too small to generate its own deep
circulatory heat

goes frigid
to hard core. Blank face

3 BYA - *moon
freezes*
registering
the scars of impacts back three billion
years. Sky's alabaster

mausoleum
quarried from earth. Preserving there last
furies of dead stars.

While here earth's own
stone pulse beats on (liquid and alive
at heart regenerative). To push out
continents
from molten trench. Inching
muscularly through depths. To crash plate
under plate. To raise
these mountain temples
jagged & ascendant with slow force
of planet manifest in them.

You feel
that sometimes walking here. Earth slips up-
ward into air

4.0 MYA - *Sierra
uplift starts*
heart-hammering
construction
shaping stone to its own
domed & spiring cathedral.

14

                                        Feel
too, deep down your own long quaking fears
release to flow of faith. That all that
moves also renews. Depths & heights in
oscillation carrying our lives
in waves to full fruition. Rounding
again as earth
                        itself back into
self subducts.
                To forge fresh surge of
mountainous ascent.

                        That pendant moon
about to set (like pearl upon gold
chain of peaks) still swims the sky as when
first formed. Stare there at spare

                                topography
of time. Then focus closer on
this living earth thrust up to frame the stars.
Sing fluent hallelujahs to our
source. Proclaim
                        all possibilities
implicit in this still emergent
universe.

Soft stone

                Feel now once more warm stone
held in your hand (like snowball you once
gathered & reshaped out mustering
new friends to play). That warmth is sunlight
come through you to touch again earth's own
warmth come from deep within—one star
conversing with itself in granite
and in flesh.

                Hot fire held within
encircling stone folds over on
itself (becoming metamorphic)—thin
film of life around us laps

flame-like
up cold mountain heights.

                    Take that to dream on
as you feel earth turn stone cold to face
night down
                    sun's fire set. This planet's
formative at heart. Forever
being born.

3.3 MYA -
current
glaciations
begin

                    Feel shivers of that truth
in boulders here you might first take
for black bears roaming night. Or remnant
drift of asteroids
                    come long last to rest.
In fact left only centuries back

13,000 YA -
latest
Pleistocene
glaciers retreat

by melting ice. This landscape's still snow-fresh.
Look right you might see sculpture here not
known before. Like temple artifacts
unfinished yet
                    inscribed with story.
Long lines incised in granite tracing
lineage that brought rock here. Stones carried
on stone river bearing down to mark
hard passages. Think ice
                    free falling
down millennia from skies piled thick
with cloud. Crystal on crystal down as if
small stars. Outreaching galaxies
come here to earth to work refinements
on tall sacred towers telling all
there is to know: Where
                    we come from. Where
we need to grow and towards what purposes.
And finally how to live—what round *earth*
ethic might best route us up unknown
hellacious slope
                    slip-knotted each
to all against sure fall off vast
deteriorating glacier

we (damnably) now face. As Muir once
avalanched
        cascading consciousness
through & into (shaping) these same peaks
same valleys
        paths & thoughts resounding
ruggedly to us. So each stone here
speaks still clear cut calligraphy of ice
(sky's own soft stone) its
                drifted glyphs piled
high in mounting revelations. As
in a dream (head resting on round ground)
your whole life
        aggregates
             accumulates
re-sorts into
        interpretations
ever new. As ink-steeped night prepares
fresh sheets of snow fresh
            dawn will write on.
In lucid stone we seek direction.

1869 - *John Muir,*
'My First Summer
in the Sierra'

June's journal: *I am alone*

Now feel 'specific gravity' of me.
What am I pulling in this day,
attracting & attracted to? I
ricochet among trees, mountains, boulders
warblers—tumbling sweet song through air—
through emptiness—like acrobat
releasing & re-grasped in brief embrace
of all of this, passed on, one hand
to next. (Slippery, awareness is.)
What am I held amidst? What holds me
here aloft? What do I hold that holds
me back again? And what let go? And
when? To keep momentum moving
forward without fear of fall. Free here

*(and now) to feel myself, sweet morning
song, my own to sing.*

                  *Got partnered with
this Mo guy out from Washington.
A lawyer yet. Some legal eagle
eating at him. Burned out. Head down on
grindstone. Bound so tight hurts me to see.*

*Wanting to compose response to Rich:
'I started out to hurt you, too, but
find here heart now opening, as petals
one by one arch back from calyx wide
to sun (as russet flesh of lily
trembles flame-like next to stream, pulsing
heart of granite garden) inviting
anxious bees their bumbling explorations—
as once your eyes would light & linger
on my skin, blouse slipped down shoulder all
to see. That's me this morning, water
rushing over stone. Just missing you.
I only know I am*
                alone.'

Jose's Song
(whole planet)

Nowadays I'm working
solar, talking everyone's
redemption. No other way
we're going to make it.

Each time I cut a length
of wood—say, reinforcing
rafters, or for blocking—
I feel my father watching
down on me like when

I was a kid. He'd all the time
be on me how when measuring
each fraction of an inch makes
all the difference. 'Measure
up,' he'd say. 'Just measure

up, before you cut.' Up here
I'm thinking he'd be out
measuring the distances
like star to star. Like when
his eyes would shine back at

me telling him these trillion
organisms crafted ocean salts
to silicon they laid down
as they died so we someday
could lay photovoltaics out

on rooftops glistening like tar
to catch fresh sunlight in
so we can read—or he could
power up his shop. Life hands
life on to other life. Each time

I put a panel down, I see that
old Apollo photo—whole planet
swimming through black night,
deep blue, awash in light we
keep returning to, each dawn

spun round. And think: Each
moment somewhere it's now
dawn, the people waking up
to do the work that must be done.

Mo's Song
(metrics)

Better believe
up on the hill
lawmakers need
their taxes done

with fine precision.
That's where I come in.
I'm *good* at it,
make it so it

adds up metrics
they want. It's laws
& numbers cause
the world grow round—

no rhyme nor reason
only bottom
line. I've bottom-
fished, I've floundered

with the best of them.
Come up for air
sometimes like here.
End up back down.

That's it. All told.
Rewrite the code.
Grow up. Grow old.
Embrace the cold.

Lily's Song
(mom gardened)

Mom gardened
all the time. Out
back brick rubble
she would turn
to beds, sweet
peas twining over
everything, deep red
tomatoes we could
eat like apples from
her hands. Must've
been some kind of
therapy I'm thinking
that black dirt she'd
sink her fingers in,
such relish & release
from all day turning
back white sheets
just so for finicky
rich folk. But what do
I know? Could just be
plain simple love
the way her fingers
felt upon my scalp
each Saturday she'd
wash my hair out, getting
ready for the week —
'No child of mine
not going to shine.'
Man came to ask,
wasn't she proud
of such a garden?
She'd look away.
(She'd say to me,
more like be humble
what earth does.)
Then just to please,
'Go on now! Mercy! Only
workers here're the bees.'

June's Invocation
(as under earth)

Face up to night, not so much to
observe, but to
let be
in you all you
can't know.

Let dark come in
where dark resides
already, back

behind bright eyes
as under earth roots move
& mycelia

do their
relentless work
connecting

everything. Let night
move miracles in you beyond
all comprehension. Then

let in the stars

for what they are, unlikely light,
learning in time

to concentrate dark
hydrogen till it
ignites.

Reach out
& stir old ember
galaxies.

Then turn yourself
to rest in darkness.

3

. . .

T*uesday*

Third fire: *Water*

Let's start again by tracing back
ancestry of ice to aftermath
of supernovae
    star collapse that
seeded current swirl of galaxy's
ingredients . rich mix
      of elements
adrift
   congregate round sun & planet
then . themselves turn inward intimate
in scale
    to interchange those energies
embedded by the stars in every
atom's structure . one with one
       another
spinning off new
      constellations
of molecular dimensions . vast
space between each
      charging particle
analogous to planetary
tracks
   harmonically revolving round
far centered sun . its needled light
       pricking
all things to grainy promise of

resounding
> life . the universe
infinitely diminutively
expounding ever
> deeper new
expansions
> on a theme.

Crystalline creation

> So water
(H$_2$O) of hydrogen (first seed
of universe) locked
> in tight embrace
with offspring oxygen

12 BYA - *oldest
detected water
molecules*

> fluidly
steps out from hot demise of stellar giants
in sparkling
> profusion & array
sun-spun across flamboyant
> fabric
of emergent time . & turns
> on dime .
ice
> crystals shimmering against
hard shining darkness—

> imagine this
strobe-lit
> wild
> choreography
of cosmos then
> slipping off thin
> trailing
gossamer . urgent &
> delicate
as fingers touch preparatory
to long-pent
> sweet cumulating
pulse of procreation—

             imagine
photons
        skating on
            thin ice
                endless
paths & patterns . laying
            down tracks
in random abandon of increasing
sheer delight . wherein
              new chemical
reactions
       instantaneously
take form
       & melt away (as
               lineage
of swirling snowstorm
                 splays each crystalline
creation
      utterly unique &
yet repeating
         infinite in
possibility) among them first
organic
      molecules . loose ends
             switching
restlessly as tail of comet.

Aggregating effervescence
           He
takes long drink of water, thinking
maybe how dendritic stream now roots
this mountain feelingly through him.

           Mass
aggregating into earth . sorts it-
self . light
       effervescent elements
upbubbling from heavy core turned

inward (gradient
of gravity
steepest at pit of planet
from which
it softens outward) . as orbits
closest
to the sun sift . moisten . round to shape
from unleavened elements
stone
planets .
while gaseous giants their light
meringues whip & concoct
far out . so
earth
with funneled force of iron &
other metals clamps down tight within
to generate intensity
of heat
enough to keep
whole planet
percolating.

Topographies of cloud

From which . all life's
eventual constituents
rise up .
carbon (bonding prolifically)
hydrogen & oxygen (pooling
to water) . nitrogen . calcium
sulfur . phosphorus .
steaming out to
vent . brown billowing topographies
of cloud
towering above all mountains
aerial terrain . foreshadowing
all landscape
malleable to passing
breath of heat or cold . shape-shifting
everything.

His fingers splash out
smattering of water onto flames.
Again. Like blessings from mercurial
font, the droplets bounce & bead & sizzle
back white steam.

           Said clouds thrust outward into
space . cool down . condensing . then first
rains . that falling
           steamily return
slow boil back to air . off heat
               layered
underneath (as round beads
               down about
her breast will swoop in lengthening
suspension (as lover hovers over
her beloved) then curve
             back up along
translucent strands . so
          rain flows down . returns
to cloud) breathing deep
            stratigraphy
of atmosphere . long eons shouldering
oceans
       held aloft
          in pendant
drops (formed & reformed) over &
again (tumbled &
          polished) each small
liquid gem .
        reflecting liquid planet
blossoming within.

4.3 BYA - crust
hardens, rains
come

Massage of gravity

          Slowly hard rains
reach deeper . inexorable massage
of gravity
        releasing . pressing
down (steam . then liquid . steam again . then back

round motions
                softening in time) to
touch long last warm peaks that rise to meet
cool fingering
                of raindrops bringing
back deep history of planet . back
to grainy
                birth . inseminated
by the stars . rounded & pressed to liquid
distillate of cosmos . earth
                                recalling
now first touch
                of gravity . as it
again . finds itself shuddering . at wet
sensation down
                hot magma stem
into pooled depths of planet's . formative
intent . now feeling
                        spilling over
its young body . all enveloping
smooth water
                recollecting . down smooth
lava floes fresh molten force . new streams
sinuously unbraiding
                        combing out
pent currents . intertwined . embedded . as
stone & water polish down
                                each other
as if one
                material . while all
the while rain also
                        slowly soaks deep
into dark interiors of rock
penetrating
                as full brush
                                strokes touch
rough canvas caringly . utterly
absorbed . dissolving

            minerals
to swim again in rich solution
etching
       earth (each atom loosening
desirous to here engrave its
signature
        cartouche) nibbling at
edges . gathering
          up strength down
crevices to pulse & pump . firm rock
imparting shape to
           water . muscular
in sure response . picking up
            speed enough
to heft sand granules to carve
& carry larger rock
        to knock
           down

mountains torrenting through clefts to round
& sculpt earth . grain
        by grain (water &
land become
      the same) as standing wave
forms . rides upon
       pure surge & rush of
turbulence . before depositing
first layer of myriad
        horizons
cumulating down through time to bear
expectant
      hills . full-bodied . at full
circle amplitude & perfect pitch
each slope reposing . as if
        music
fluidly expressed of parent stone
& aggregated pull of full
       earth

bearing down on rounding curvature
of universe .
                              through which . softly
resonant (as after love . one drifts
towards sleep) deep
                              lowland river moves past
hills (rounding & rounded in return)
returning
                    always (ever in quest
of planet's center) stone to steeped
fluidity . all things
                              towards ocean womb—
as large snake slowly takes
                              warm mammal
in its coils . tightening each breath . as flesh
of one becomes the other.

Ocean's conversation

                              Lead gray
the gathering waters spread . earth's matte
emulsion holding in gestation
rich particulates . flat

4.3 BYA –
oceans form

                              photographic
plate awaiting light . inked lexicon
anticipating breath
                    to stir it
into life . thus
                    newly fluent earth
convenes all elements to join
ocean's incessant
                    conversation .

and from thin stratospheric latticework
of snowflakes
                    dancing at far interface
of earth's & sunlight's radiant
embrace . lacy . long-
                    strung-out flagellate
organic molecules now tumble

down
       to merge with oceans teeming with
profuse ingredients . and

             into
these new seas from deep space comets plunge
new depths
         delivering
              continually
carbon & ice . steaming
            trainloads
pounding down to pull of planet's heart
to melt in unison . and from
              each such
encounter . billions of
           small globes dance
out all directions . swirling within
these swelling seas . while

            underneath . earth
ever still exudes slow churn of stone's
own circulation
        welling up . heart
magma pulsing . wave-like . out new
continents
      to dive again dissolving
to return all rock to melt into
new
      generations . earth itself renewed
re-blossoming . thus fresh
          as reddest
rose or petals of white surf left wet
on sand . or dreams
         released from lucid
sleep fluidly to sculpt the waking
world . all things
       sing one long song.

Storm's cauldron
                                        Likewise
above . mercurial skies coil
constantly . uplifting
                        drifting
continents
                    of air laced through with
earthen elements . through which like pearl
on irritant
                    within an oyster's
churning musculature . occasionally
the sun
                    burns down . its wavering light
transformed on touching atmosphere
to heat (each stroke
                        down curvature of
earth exciting differentially
each
            molecule to motion
                                    up &
down . gyration on . long shivering
shafts) coupling in
                        turbid . slow
convection with whole planet's heat
                                            surging
beneath (and roll of mutual
gravitational
                    attractions) stirring
sun & earth to spawn
                        vast storm .

                                        high clouds
rain down acidic mix . eating at
stone . winds

                    whip high seas relentlessly
send
            marshaled waves marching against sheer
continents . deep

                   churn of sand at gut
of each surge letting loose last roar
then sigh & rattle .

                   high & wide . sheet
lightning
            encases everything in
cannon fire
            glaze & gauze
                        of light . like
white
         cocoon or shroud ablaze.

Electric touch
                              At that
electric touch of fissured sky . or
fingering of magma
                  steaming jet
black ink of ocean depth
                        milk white (with
kaleidoscopic tint of elements
released again
               from core) . from shock of such
enormity of energy on
oceans
          now alive with chemical
potential . new
               molecules are
forged . new compounds pounded out to more
complex
         organics . *amino acids*
lengthening long interactive lines left
dangling (as if
               to catch some
other line
          adrift) or *lipids*
circling back in on self (one end
of each constituent
                  molecule

averse to solvent water dives
away . the other
                    end left facing
out to fuse protective sphere
                              against
tempestuous world) much as (much
later) musk ox herd
                    turns outward lowered
crescent horns . to form one solid ring
cradling
          soft calves within . while through
white arctic storm
                    circle white wolves intent
their own pups must be fed.

Two oceans
                              Absent-
mindedly he stirs hot tea, its steam
white currents also circling.

                              So also .
telescoping time . a second line
of lipid molecules
                    forms to face
that smaller sea held round within
first sphere . perfecting
                              membrane to define
inside from out . interior
from one's environment . and more
                              than that
permit some chosen elements to
pass
          (benefiting interactions
stirring within) or issue out
(resultant toxins) .
                    fluidity
so concentrates within
                    thin lens . in

focused
        actions fostering
                new
possibilities . earth now can choose
its own directions .
             two oceans now
two spheres inhabit . one a planet .
another (molecular) nested
within.

Chemical transcendence

      Now differentially new
proteins grow (twisting
              amino
acids lanyard-like to Protean
giant compounds) responsive to
                changing
conditions
        inside & out—and then
begin themselves to change conditions
(inside & out)—and
           then . themselves again
changing in
        interaction . find
finally fortuitous feedback
loops sustaining
         those conditions most
conducive to their own
            continuing
reactions (bringing in . disposing
what's needed & what's not) . thus

               proteins
(within encapsulating lipid
membranes) spin
        forth small bubbles of
stability . exponentially
successfully securing chemical

transcendence in
                    the midst of storm (as
eye of storm itself forms steady pearl
of calm within
                    wild turbulence) .

4.0 BYA - *life
forms on earth*

thus
        always
                fluidity
                        so rounds
itself to structure . as earth first did
mid sea
        of gravity . or tear
turned inward . glistening . will hold
full story
            bursting to be told.

Catching last light
                        So much
so that . as storm diminishes
production of complex
                        molecular
entrapment of raw energies—earth
cooling to quiescence . no longer
stirring . cooking . serving up
                        fine ready
mix of star-enriched ingredients
to fuel first life—life . sputtering
exhausts
            its resources and layers down
in its trillions (so successful had it
been compounding increase of consumption)
toward abysmal rest . faint
                        starry
asterisks to planet's death.

                        *He spreads
the embers, douses down outliers,
settles in as if all night to wait*

the fire out, watch
            coals, one by one, flick
off to leave cold stars alone in their
eternity (though also fading
finally) or else keep vigil prayer
to stir warm dawn.

            But that one molecule
(minuscule within small solo sphere)
in one
            blind flash of inspiration
instantaneously
                  conceives
                        how best
to
      catch
            one
                  photon
                        zinging
                              past
                                    at
speed of light direct
                  from sun
                        & take
& hold it in . absorbing impact
shimmering
            like long-bow arrow
shot across high arc from dawn of time
unquivering
            full force
                  long last
                        to meet
that one
            pearled dewdrop (giving back steeled glint
of bull's eye) entering immaculate
immensity—
                  from which . regrouping . time
again now forward haltingly

3.9 BYA – *life
here invents
photosynthesis*

unfurls (wave-like
>>>>>>swimming in tight
font) converting
>>>>>>energy of star
to stir of life within one cell
risen again .
>>>>so life renewed
re-radiates that moment on to you.

June's journal: *My medicine*

Stardust or not, I'm coated with it—
sepia of stuff kicked up by journey
jamming every pore—feel caked & cratered
frozen-faced as shady lady moon
revolving—dance of diva painted
with ground pigments, ratcheting archaic
footage through old-time projector—
imagery not meant for me. I want
it off, want cold
>>>>>>*stream burning clean—down*
to the bone—pure snowmelt muscling
my flesh downstream, scouring white skin
smooth as granite—as flame—as polished
surface of swift water—sheen on stone
all that remains of me.
>>>>>*So find*
myself spread-eagled late this morning
hugging hard to belly boulder big
almost beyond my grasp, its curvature
that of the earth. I press heart deep through
rock to pulse of water pounding all
around. Then thought
>>>>>>*returns, 'Physician, heal*
thyself, heal heart of planet.'
>>>>>>*Sun then starts*
slow work massaging back its warmth
through me, and then again, through me to stone.

Gwen's Song
(emergent)

Emergent
from lake feel
elemental
walk
up slant of
stone slight swagger
upright (& of
breast) then touch
fingertips to
steepness teetering but
bold dripping
new as if
first time to move
through earth
as through
high treetops
feel
arch of
foot grip rock
then find flat spot
arch back
to perfect
fit
right angle
to the sun
straight down
on every
part of me
at once yet
separately to lift
each droplet
from bare skin
into warm air
breeze toweling
what's left
eyes close
& scarlet
veils layer
inward twirling

intertwine
rough grain
of granite
earth stretched out
every direction round
horizons
round sun round
planet
hot & red within.

Meru's Song
(model mtn.)

build memory
to model
mtn.

connect ea.
(mtn.) moment
in 2 us.

pan & pixillate
ea. seen
grain
like manna
I communicate
snowed
down from
heaven.

whole planet
we so
have & hold—
earth's emergent
nervous system—
all us
this
capable

2 b o
not.

Vince's Song
(return)

I feel like I'm not whole
no more—like that I've seen
too much, too soon. Don't want
to talk about it none.
Here it's all great, man, sun
stone, trees, the stream, the air.
I feel free here, know what
I mean. They say we fight
for this but I don't see it.
Aren't no big word pledge
allegiances out here.
Just friends. Just breathe, just be
and let be free. Let live.
That's it. Let live. Things die
enough without us at
it too, fall naturally
like leaves do. Damn raven
bombing acorns shook me
up, man. I'm raising fist
into the air shaking
at him. So he comes down
starts grinding husks against
the stone (like Indian
like me). Looks eye to eye
like 'Man what's up with *you*
afraid of *me*? Get real. Unless
you dead or something, then
but then who cares? Just put
you back in service, back
in circulation, way I
see it.' I'm laughing at
myself, think sure he'd first
go after eyes & such, sweet
meats inside the nut. I've
seen life pecked
apart, like every day, back
there like desert sand gets in
your eyes, or what do they

say 'smoke' of
battle? Just eats
at you. I stretched out
on the rock, buck naked
felt hard rush of water
pounding past. It took my
breath with it downriver
mingling forever
& wherever. Felt cold spray
peck flesh away
return me to my senses.

Jose's Song
(fish parable)

Hey man you
hear the one?

Give a guy a fish
he eats a day.

Teach him to fish he eats
the fishery.

Lily's Song
(mud puddle world)

I gather round
the little ones
in sound of just
my voice (shut down
all other noise)
return to source
inside us—where
the earth speaks up.

I listen to one
child again
another chiming in
the way wind will
all else gone still.
Nothing profound.
Just music all around.

And rounder, then,
the wonder in
their eyes. Like tree
rings growing large
in time of rain
(unless too long
this desert widens).

Let me their tear
of moisture be—
one raindrop diving in
round pool to touch
& circle out from
center to embrace
mud puddle world
grown infinite.

Marta's Song
(Cycladic)

I was inspired first time
happening on white
Cycladic goddess in
our garden, where mother
(quite devoted to old
ways) had placed her to hold
sway over narcissus—
'paperwhites' she called them.

From that spring day I knew
I'd sculpt. It was the touch
of almost breathing stone
seemed to inseminate
in me desire to reach
down my hands into such
hardness, kneading it like
dough, to shape, bake, break,

pass round to feast us all
on its sweet sustenance.
Last summer I went back
to Paros, where fine-grained
crystalline white marble
veins deep earth, yielding its
flesh-soft translucence
to sculptresses spread round

the wide encircling
Mediterranean.
I wanted to get to
the heart of it—take off
(as told) my daypack, leaving
it to mark sole entry of
old shaft, and then descend
far in as I can go

(earthquake, I'm thinking, whole
way back). But stay with it.
Sit facing face of stone.

Douse light. Become silence
of stone, deep breathing dark
interior of stone, womb
where stone dreams stir. There
I still go when stuck what

to do next, stone being
unforgiving. Most days
though, it's play, like skipping
smooth, flat cobbles over
waves near shore (where ocean
spins each marbled rock to
fit of fingers lifting it
to throw) to meet, just

so, incoming surf with
stone's own slow momentum
held within. Whole islands
sea so sculpts. Then no one's
much surprised to pull from
her new Aphrodites
shaped as we've always known
her beauties had to be.

Marta's Lament
(pearls)

Pearls at my breast
like trace of foam
left by slow lap
of waves on sand—

your touch, too, left
impressions here
I search all day
remembering—

full days I sculpt
in marble now
such roundness found
too hard to bear.

45

Mo's Dream
(Cassandra)

This oil tanker
named Cassandra
comes sailing perfect
storm of calm
through pitch black
night straight at
that iceberg
everyone knows
must be there, calved
off ice cap in shrieks
as shatter steel — long
running crack through
air, through acid sea
incurably transmitted
on through ship, as if
the planet (atom-like)
were readying to split.
Just do the math.
It's only now a matter
of hard time. We call
the bridge, get back
the same old static
music looping. Sheer
helplessness spreads
through whole crew.
And me. Sheer nothing
here to do. Who
was it didn't trust
the call from, was it
Kawela, that dark dawn
(on whose instruction?)
radar scanning waves
of fighters screaming in
plain prophecies of
one more noble war?
What if they'd listened?
What if they'd made
a different calculation?

I watch sea as it wakes
white streaming ghosts
astern, as we go on
full-steam, damn everything.

June's Song
(metrics)

Wonder:
must be more
bacteria

than stars—
just here
on earth—

on me—
in
their

trillions—
universe
on

nested
universe
expanding—as

my heart
each beat each
breath.

Gwen's Song
(memory)

Memory
of sun is
all it is—
electrons
packed in
lithium
tight as you
can get, then
each cell too
wherever
there's more
room, but kept
low down
to center
gravity
for handling
the curves.

I tell them
every battery's
a mile more
you can go.
Just think you're
traveling
on starlight
(take that in)—
stow starlight
tight enough
you'll travel
far as dawn—
(I tell them
purring
quietly)
give me
the memory,
I'll drive you
to the moon.

No different
from
metabolism
slowly we
are learning
what earth's
been learning
all along.
Conversion
I am preaching—
sweet
road up to
salvation,
plugged into
everlasting
sun.

Earth lasts
without us.
That's our
choice—to be
here or not—
& how much
damage in
our sorry
name remains.

Each day
I drive down
Wilshire past
the tar pits,
herds of us
as stuck
as condor
flapping oiled
wings above
carcass of
full-coated
mastodon.
We labor in
delusion
to be free.

I drink
the Kool-aid
same as
everyone—
'Petroleum
Primates' we
call ourselves
yanking
out the guts
of cars. Trust
me these hands
aren't ever
coming clean—
but that
the earth still spins
electron-like
within
old timer
carburetor
mind.

4

.

. . .

Wednesday

Fourth fire: *Fire*

*He holds his hands up, fingers slightly
cupped to fire's radiance, receiving
warmth of wood, so many summers'
days wrapped tight within round annual rings
releasing now to night, like church bells
ringing out embrace of sound, now held
again in touch, his rounding hands like
sculptor's laid on pulsing, breathing air
responding to slowly revolving
heat. He holds warmth there a moment. Then
turns palms up to sting of starlight singing
down as if in resonance within
hand-polished grail.*

                        Feel that one

                                   photon

first triggering photosynthetic
life Take that

                 back first

                       to sun—

                                   one

atom

        (hydrogen)

                  spun from

                         (one each)

electron encircling proton

which in heat
massively
strips down bare
protons fused in thermonuclear
reaction
spawned by sheer preponderant
gravity of trillions
more such
atoms letting loose pure
energy first
stored in their
tight orbits at the start
of time

Elixir of all things

*He stops to warm himself again
as if caressing sun.*

Keep pressing
back that energy through radiant
lineage of stars
one generation
imploding down to next
Reverse
radiance into compression
as if
this heat
increasing
as you
move
hand in toward flame went on increasing
exponentially intensity
Feel it
at fingertip
sharp energy
of everything compressed to less &
less
space as space

itself (& time)

contracts

back into

unitary origin

He adds logs, fire licking at them, circling
as cat will do to find right spot on
lap, then settle in.

This universe

exploded

everywhere at once since

everywhere was then

one

speck

13.7 BYA - *'Big*
Bang' creates
time & space

This fire

one could say was (and

is) the center

of said cosmos

Take that in

Right here

we're

at the start & future of

creation

So

then

now

begin

to add back in

all else

to this

ringed space—

more logs whole forests these stones
containing fire whole mountains oceans
earth itself all organisms all
your memories—

fed back into these
flames
　　　not losing mass or energy
but honed to pure
　　　　　elixir of all things
Imagine
　　　fire dense & hot enough
to hold all this within
　　　　　this one stone
circle Then
　　　add the sun
　　　　　bring down round sky
of stars all galaxies and every
energy
　　　unseen now into
single
　　　flame
　　　　　condensing
　　　　　　　then again
to solitary
　　　spark
　　　　　unfathomed
singularity

Needling of quarks

　　　Long silence as
the embers talk among themselves
considering.

　　　So concentrate
(all time)(all space) here now
　　　　　so penetrate
pure nothingness
　　　　　pin-
　　　　　　　prick
　　　　　　　　in
　　　　　　　　　which
　　　　　　　　　　　blinks

out
infinity
all
vanishing

that
@
that

point

bounds boundlessly entire

fire
flaring back full force
pent infinite
to spire
spike
spoke forth
concurrent with

out-shining tracks of time irradiant
through
endless new
expanse

Feel needling

of*quarks*firstpoppingin&outof
being(uncorkedtheuniverse
intoxicatedwithitself,giddy
atmerefactofitsexistence
poursforthsheerbubblyprofusion
drinkingdeepatdeepestsource)feel*quarks*
thensoberingto*protons/neutrons*
oscillatingintightjostleof
neutrinos.allthisasrumbling
proceedseruptionrushingforthone

fullsecond(alleternity)then
everybillionofonebillionone
photon-born*electrons*'annihilates
with'*positrons*floodingwholeuniverse
with*light*—particulatedphotons
packedsotightwithinconstrictedspace
*light*tripsuponremnantelectrons
agitatingenergy&matter
pitch&mixsothickitfirstburnsblack
(unflickeringflameno*light*escapes)

      .

Opaque as poppy seed

Opaque
          as poppy seed all being
nucleated deep within that round
gestation the universe expands
from speck 400,000 years till
light relaxing wavelength into ampling
space softens its tempestuous pitch
to swelling chords invoking charging
progeny electrons to secure
safe haven round firm ground of protons there
to found first stable structure in
first atoms—hydrogen, helium
& lithium—matter arising from
long coiling storm of fire taking fire
in tight coiled bonds bright rings encircling
like candlelight on altar pulsing
central to (at heart of) vast cathedral
being built of it So now each
atom harbors store of energy
to light all futures And now first light
that nursed whole glowing structure into
place at last stems
                forth in
                    pyrotechnic

13.6996 BYA –
first atoms form

staminate
outburst
full flowering
through spaciously transparent universe
its glory
plain to see

Relic of light

He spreads orange
flickering embers evenly, their
warmth upwelling
into us.

Reach out
to touch the warmth of that first fire
burning still before us now
burning
within our each creation blossoming
through flesh
each step you take each day you
wake into rose-fingering embrace
of dawn unfurled
in readiness We live
at iris-ragged edge of but one
oceanic universe
outswelling
bellowing perimeter of flame—
of time—
that overtakes each instant
mere eternal emptiness
as pin-
prick morning light first stirs in you far fires
of creation raging new

Here by
this fire opening to universal
fire—pond of lotus brimming—soft
eyes walk over burning coals, sharp chop
of radiance, sharp petals each its

instance of eternity. I see
my instant, too, soft petal flesh &
consciousness in
                                    time-lapse
                                                bloom.

                                            Relic
of that primordial light long banked
& long since traveling (13.
7 billion
                    years) reverberates
right here
                    right now
                                    throughout
                                                all space its
photons
                    (layered in lengthening universe)
teased out to microwaves
                                    we still hear
hiss in
                    headphones—as you hear here this
fire's breath expire Stretched
                                    out tonight as
you roll over
                    and look up (from deep
dream into consciousness
                                    arising)
you'll see each time
                                    you wake stars ratchet
further round
                    vast silver web
                                            earth spins
on polar point
                    far north (got hold there
of tail of *ursa minor* little
bear) as planet
                    rolls & lumbers
through long course (dark
                                    universe therein

also awakening
            from grainy
depths to bright recurrent dream then
                                    daily
lucid blossoming)

                Then notice too
another point of light
                put there by us
apparently unmoving
                just so
we can talk like this
                familiarly
at any distance
                Listening to
first such
        satellite we heard as well
(circa ancestral 1960s)
whisper   1965 – *Penzias &*
        of universe awakening   *Wilson detect*
in us   *microwaves from*
                                           Big Bang
        dim understanding of
its birth and
                like long-separated
family conversing
                over time
wide-eyed our own birth
                    too begin to
comprehend We send
                for photographs
receive back finally   1989 – *NASA*
                                           maps 'cosmic
            deciphered   *background'*
pixilated confirmation (like   *microwaves*
old
        shroud that hints divinity)
revealing first burst
                    of light already
showing full
            impregnate structure of

whole universe we see around us
every day
              its tissued synapses
where galaxies will be

Universe in utero

                              Light's long
gestation under
              wrap of random
particles had let
              dark matter
come to term
              coagulate to pull
of its own gravity to grow enough
to slow
              expanding universe
in spots so space there
                              pockets
                                            back
on self re-curving to
                              anomalous
dark density deep
              self-reflective
mystery
              Here matter newly
structured into atoms
              (& so
freed too from light's incessantly
intense caress
              now carrying light's
energy within) begins
              also
to coalesce
              its newfound mass and
gravity at play

              Space bends again
at that increasing
              weight (time slows in

the direction
            of our own round
moment) as if the universe
in utero
            set out to form next
generation of
            fecund creation—
heavy with helium
            & hydrogen
now rounding in
            on self to spark (on
forge of pounding gravity) first stars
rekindling
            those fires banked
within first atoms to release
                        again
free light
            resuming the construction
of new elements down progeny
of more stars
            dropping like raindrops from
dark billowing expansive clouds
returning then
            to form & drop again
stars in their trillions spattering
across
            9,000,000,000 years
                        before one
sun starts measuring
                        eventually
to spin that single photon here
to spark
            on earth new birth of then
sustaining
            generations
                        down to us.

13.3 BYA –
stars form

June's journal: *Namaste*

Ironclad sky melts ferrous into dawn:
Sing hallelujah now red flow
resumes—cold sickle moon hung still, night's
harvest done. Return
                              now to clear day
once more, slowly lengthening ascent
of light out to pure empty blue
of space, spare consciousness of all one might
encompass & accomplish.
                              Still deep
inside me molten possibilities
churn over, hot & heavy, who knows
what or how might be?
                              So serious
he is these days, just needing me
to be all he can
                              imagine, perfect
trajectory—damn jets he's flying
in his head, projecting us out there
to win
            security by other
means. While here, ascendant
                              flame, high sun
steadies & strengthens into me, entire
earth resplendent and respondent
as body cradled in its touch.
                              So
day sloughs off the dark.
                              I lean back safe
& comfortable as cotton I
unbutton
            opening to let fresh
air brush over me as if a painting,
glaze on glaze of sunlight, over &
again, as skin refocuses each
touch and nuance of warm medium

connecting us—gone one with sun, wide
radiant creation.
                    Beside me
on hard stone then slowly pump thin wings
of Mourning Cloak, like hands that come
together, Namaste. 'I bow down
to the god in you.' Namaste,
I breathe into this pulsing moment—who—
are—you—now come to be with me—angel-
winged—dark forest-velvet-fringed-gold
radiance? Whom do
                         we mourn if not
ourselves lost to such fluttering
transformation? Let caterpillar past
peel off, this clear day my chrysalis.
Learn now to dance together up through
buoyant air.
                First
                         here
                              soak in the sun,
nurse rock of mineral, then circle
me in further search of all—we—need.
Moth-like, fan in me
                    deep flame. Land here
soft wings & kiss away salt tear.

Gwen's Dance
(as flame, as stream,
as ash, as breeze)

I'll dance
as slender
flame
aspiring
to touch

of air
of sky
of sun
from which
I come —

my lover
now the earth
I settle on
as fire
circles

wick —
like water
then, quick
doused
to rivulet

descending
over stone,
transformed
to speak
sporadic

clarity —
or ash-like to
new seed
released
to air

to drift
to writhe
to rise
smoke-like
to germinate

somewhere
far breezes
whisper for
me only, me
alone

to hear—
there, darkly
I descend,
take root
again

in you—
in everything
in flame
ignited
here within.

Meru's Love Song
(I am)

i am
bic flic
the
start

of stars
of love
of all
this
:

match
me
together
we

repeatedly
star struck
burn up
burn

down burn
night long
into
dawn
!

Miwok Creation Song
(Vince)

Silver fox is lonely
so she says to great coyote
'let's sing into existence
let's sing into the night sky
let's sing up into high moon
all creation.'

Coyote says 'let duck
go dive down in deep ocean
bring me some earth
up from the bottom there
up first time into air
all creation.'

So silver fox and gray
coyote sang & danced
black night away—
with rain & seed &
drumming feet shaped slippery
earth to song

till rainbow dawn unblankets
all creation.

Marta's Song
(nest)

O how
round cosmos
holds itself
in spin

in nest,
in egg,
in embryo,
in eye

of mother
bird that tends,
rolling her
oblong orbs

to warm
just so—
all's woven
to if not

perfection
something
closer to
the earth

we know—
more open,
more
our own

sweet song
of ever
wakening
creation.

Mo's Fire Dance
(come dawn)

i.

Moses on the mountaintop
keeps warm around the burning bush.

All night he spirals, dancing there
impatient for directions to appear.

Delirious, he sees all writ
on clouds, on high skies realized—

first bellowed infinite expanse
then dissipating emptiness

sheer out of sight, of thought, of cosmos
feverish with dream of us

in & out of substance shivering,
his mind dispenses everything,

dispensed itself to atoms, drop
by drop, tock-tick, of grandma clock.

What memories, what auguries
we thread at last—but first through eye

of needle, eye of storm must pass,
let ride whatever waves now rise.

ii.

Come dawn the sky ignites again
revealing how the cosmos spins.

Ecstatic and exhausted then
I write it down as best I can

and travel down the mountainside
still wondering how to describe

the dance that holds creation close,
the laws encircling the soul—
the glory spun beyond control.

Mo's Song
(spider stars)

High spider
stars
slow crawling
drop

on silver
strands
to weave one
deep

into their
dreams,
each satin
touch

urging us
awake &
then asleep
again. All night

I count
their shuttlings
like sands
downpouring

over me.
So she
who someday
loves me

somewhere
spins
alone within
far circling.

June's Song
(2 snakes)

Amazing grace
2 snakes
make love,
heads held above
tall grasses, bodies
weaving—as with
wind—impulses
stemming from
the ground now
breathing under
me, my breath
caught up
anticipating.

I step within
long labyrinth.
I follow for awhile
how earth will
replicate itself
occasionally
in twining passions
plain to see, how
pleasure circles
out from galaxies
to touch me, sweep
me off cyclonically
toward spiral-horned
oblivion.

And when
the music dwindles
to a note, the snakeskin
dries to interwoven
scales of nothingness
the breezes blow,
I will still know
the song goes on.
The grasses always
now will sing

to push of muscle rippling
as sacred coils
make way unseen.

June's Hymn
(cathedral)

Come here for life's
enlargement—as lake becomes

the sky, and mountain
whole earth rumbling round

sun, and every tree high spire
of still cathedral. Be still

small hummingbird on wing
vibrating granite crystalline

where water dances off from
stone to spin pure sunlit air

alive above oblivion.

5

.

.   .   .

.

Thursday

Fifth fire: *Air*

Air tonight not stirring otherwise
he breathes into incipient fire, down
on all fours, like dragon cuddling
hot nothings. Fire simmering like nest
of gold awakens from round lair
of rock.

        That alchemy of sunlight
life now stirs within it (stirred in turn
by touch outreaching from
                     first moment
of creation) . bubbles
               oceans
separating . waters
           back to
hydrogen (to bake . with carbon
carbohydrate sugars) &
                 oxygen
in excess popping up to air . waste
product toxic
           to long anaerobic
fermentation processes . by which
life early-on converts
             said sugars

2.9 BYA - *oxygen*
crisis builds

back to energy (as still goes on
in guts & airless
                    seepages of swamps).

Life simmering

First safe from its own waste beneath calm
seas . that once
                    tumultuously from
breaching magma . diving meteors .
streaming electric
                    storms . convected
winds high-pitched . had churned
                                    molecular
complexities to generate &
feed first life . life
                    now itself . its life-lines
hitched direct to sun . simmers within
then out across
                    whole oceans boiling
with life . planet & star
                            thus entering
revitalized relationship . recharged .
new chemistry
                    between them sparking
(you know perhaps this feeling) . like lover
earth . now slowly . turns herself
                                each instant
towards long touch of light . one all-embracing
dawn extending
                    endlessly it seems .
sunrise eternally . caressing
cell by cell
                her every . atom stirred
in warmth & deepening response
awakening
                forever . new
transfiguration.

Earth's membrane
A billion years .
like love slow simmering . elliptically
the dance goes on . photons
                                       popping loose
stray . interactive oxygen .

                          Wind
picks up, low fire crackling suddenly
to life.

            the way this fire builds itself
from wind . oxygen . mounts into air
(plumed serpent first extending
                                  its clawed
wings) ascending
                    stratosphere
                                  where waves
of ultraviolet light . incoming .
thicken it
              to ozone . sun-screening
deleterious effects of further
ultraviolet . thus from

2.5 MYA – *ozone*
layer forms

                    within thin
membranes (bubbles bubbling each minute
atoms
            in their trillions) life constructs
earth's second crust . raising
                          up
                              high
canopy of air . planetary
membrane (earth organism . formative
within) swaddling
                      protectively
as dragon's wings enveloping whole
planet . dragon's
                    own . its glistening

gold hoard . slow pulsing . energetic clutch
of untold
          dragons . yet unhatched.

Earth burns

                            Bright
fire shifts reptilian legs—logs sloughing
off resplendent scales—awakening—fierce
ember eyes alive.

                      Proliferating
down below . fire-hissing
                         oxygen
(mere afterthought of photosynthesis)
now roams
              earth's surface far & wide
reacting with each element . its
hyperactive atoms
                anxious to
attach . freewheeling . whirling dervishes
spinning electron
              spokes . to fit (fixed
on acquiring) whatever they
first touch . lizard-
            like . quick
                   atoms flick
electron tongues . flames fast consuming
life from which they came . earth
                burns in
residue of life . oxidation
penetrating
           every crevice . crust
rusts orange . as embers flaking from burnt
wood . slowly insistent
             oxygen
unbuttoning . each molecule it
meets . to stitch
          new oxides into
earth's disheveled fabric.

Dragon's teeth

He feeds more
logs to flames now snapping to attention
flag-like, hungering for heaving wind,
all of us then shifting
                    nervously.

Life cowers from the force it has released .
most fermentation ceasing within
reach of air . cells boil
                    dry . their membranes
desiccated by . sharp searing tooth
of toxin . aerating snarl
                    of surf
curled-lipped . gnawing
                    at continents . works
down through water's marrow
                    poison . air
there mixed & masticated by cold
currents . penetrating . deep
                    life's best
sun-columned . water-sheened . shimmering
& polished palaces . that dance pure
light . through
                    darkening layers . all photons
dissipating . where
                    life buries
self . sealed off from over-burdening
of its own waste . but
                    also from fresh
sun . and thus (resourceless once again)
reverts to stark subsistence on
descending
                    carcasses
                    piled up . then
dwindling . while

                    all the while relentless
oxygen . like far-flung seed . fans down

its fibrils to root &
                    rummage something
new through deep debris.

Life burns within
                         Equally
tenacious . life erects last-ditch . thin
makeshift barricades against
                              invasion .
engaging . then intense . atom to
atom . combat in
                    defense of
flickering . long-cherished processes
caught up in
                    firestorm of aerial
assault . resistance
                    never breaking
down . goes further underground . extends
then . tentatively
                    olive-branch-like
reach to errant . captive
                         oxygen .
to coax it in . work out . increasingly
complex
            arrangements . possibilities
like dancers in a room . all atoms
swirling & yet . each
                    able to maintain
place & grace . conversing even (even
to exacting
                orchestration) .
clarifying .
            intrigues & attractions
only glanced before . and in the end
all thoroughly warmed
                    within . hard breathing .
ready to rest . yet . charged . expectant
of what dance comes next . so
                         oxygen

enthralled in life's designs . attaches
where it had attacked . and
                              life . in turn .
adapting to contain
                    those sizzling
atoms passed like hot potato . bond
to bond . finds in time . more
                          energy
released in each exchange
                        than former
fermentation could yield up . freshly
aerobic
            respiration . phoenix-
like . ascends from living flame . life
burns within
                empowered to reclaim
entire planet . striking fresh refrain
in its own image . spinning
                          out long
chains of interaction . glittering
like gold to pulse of skin
                        the moment that
the music starts again.

2.4 BYA *- aerobic
respiration
evolves*

Breathe deep

                    Rhythmically
*soft-feathered flames push up through air—blue
quetzalcoatl stirring there, blues
music set to cinema—abstract of
unfolding life
            of light.*

                    Breathe deep
the breath of pine & fir . still building here
near timberline . thin atmosphere
sustaining all our lives .
                        that meteor's
downwhooshing . bright . demise burns out to
scouring & spark of oxygen

that taken in
             each breath ignites
in you new life . trace that hot fire through
your depths . first feeling
                          reach of air
along long
           streams within your lungs
dendritic as terrain of mountains
evening breezes now
                    wash down .
                                 restore
yourself . take rest
                     between each breath
exchanging there burnt carbon for fresh
oxygen . absorbed . then swept
                               off into
ocean . pounding . steadily . at heart
iron-strong (now oxidated
                          red) to
pulse & drum to far horizons . air .
to stir with care
                  those fires . coloring
like sunrise
             ancient seas still riding
deep within each cell & person . feel
there (spiraling
                 like solar system)
blazing atoms . radiance of stars
dance to your purposes . breathe and
                                     connect
to all of this . one interaction
fanned to lasting
                  life . breathe deep and know
how far the universe in you aspires .
breathe deep & listen long
                           to your deep song.

June's journal: *Mom dream*

I'm walking with you all last night again
the way we did along flat beach last
time we were together, my small hand
enveloped in your sureness, mother,
walking final sands—your cancer
teeming exponentially and me
about to burst from childhood into
empty universe. You said, 'I am
here always sure

                        as dream.' So still we're
walking all this morning up last mountain
once again, the twin-peaked one, your voice
within the wind curling like breakers
over cedar shores. You said, 'Look for
the ocean everywhere you go.
I will be with you then.'

                         So here thin
air burns into, buffets me, each step
just colder, eyes stung nearly shut with
force of it, yet gasping up and up
for breath, drowning in insufficiency.
What if

              life isn't meant to be
at height like this? What if I'm not
able to get back by dark, cold gnawing
me already down to bone? I stop
to shelter among rocks, nursing last
nourishment. Then spot snow-pack, beach-like,
crawling with—

                    ladybugs!—they gather
here you said this time of year—as moth
will gyre up towards moon to one specific
height to meet

                  right mate. (I look around
still nothing doing.) Laugh

                        out loud: to think
so all alone, then, no, especially

up here (life contralto-ing) I am
my own warm tide pool swarming what
might be, small quote of ocean lifted up
to shine from mountaintop hot beacon
pulse of sun.

                    I summit and start down,
no time to waste, deliberately each
step placed
                on angled rock, as if
this mountain were
                      this cubist sculpture
                                shaped
by gravity—and me one moving
part of it. Like mountain now I root
each foot, in balance, holding self erect
as compass-point precisely trained to
heart of earth. So love—of earth, of
anything & anyone—must move
in me, responsively to larger
force. So you hold me, mother, as mountain
rides up over continent from sea
on magma earth
                      relentlessly at birth.

Mother, this gift I am of you, each
second lived, each breath exchanged, my life
this mountain chipped by ocean air—each
raindrop, ice-pick-snowflake driven hard
by gravity again & freeze & wind
encircling the planet. So let me
sculpt each day my life—and in small part
the life of earth, growing in me—each
round, wondrous moment to give birth
to further possibility.
                    So
breathing easily, cross-country free,
spiraling
                from mountain I descend.

Vince's Song
(mountain)

You know
you never know
what difference
does it make.

Like some nutcase
blasts Crazy Horse
from mountain face.
That's great. I mean

if that's the way
you want you spend
your life. But what
would Crazy Horse

who died there
(and his people like
tall prairie grasses)
have to say?

Which way does
the wind go walking
making waves today?
That song I'd like

to hear, that whispering
I'd like to sing.
Then let it be.
Let air carve

mountain quietly.

Marta's Song
(dead trees sculpt)

Dead trees sculpt white
smoke rising from
dried land
white

cemetery
statuary or bleached coral
sun swims through
emptily

where once bright schools
revealed prismatic
truth

light
has in it
once given chance
to live—once
oceanic
air

flicks aspen
gold
again.

Jose's Song
(be true)

Dad said: 'Be
true unto the tree.'

Follow the grain
where it leads you.

True up each edge
to fit the thing

you have in mind
to build, fit that

to what the tree
would want to be.

Honor the life
given for you

to hold in hand
to finish, and

when done, pass on.

Gwen's Song
(sweet)

How sweetly
earth extracts
itself
through flowers
into air
where, breathing
deep, I take
in all
her
essences
as if
dispensed
direct
from
greenest
stem till
like bright
blossom
I too
open, close
again
around
whole earth
I carry
now within
like seed
I give
new birth.

Meru's Prayer
(let spirit)

Let spirit
flow
as wind
as water
shaping
over

every-
thing in
constant
act of
one
creation.

Let light
so flow
and earth
under
its touch
& influence.

Let life
in me
and all
of us
so grow —
and love

so touch.

June's Song
(Lepidopteran)

She flits to
land briefly
among leaves,
becoming
one. Except
the wings pulse
still. Bellows
are they, pulling
in sweet air
to abdomen?
Or solar
sails absorbing
near star's
warmth? Rhythmically
they work,
certainly as if
to purpose.
As if some
musculature of
thorax, even
resting, must
find use. Beauty,
I think, will so
express. Or prayer
its own bright
semaphore
to heaven
send. I bring
flat palms together
at the chest. Ah, be
& stay, light
touch of
memory. Ah, to
so open and so
close
to brush of wings
here visiting —
to song
she sings.

Mo's Song
(every breath)

Sitting streamside, sun
streams down
through air, air every
breath streams in, then
out, connecting
me with this

mountain at rest,
dreaming granite.
I break
dry matzoh, place
on tongue, cleansing
taste — unleavened

I am
traveling light.
Want nothing but
what is
right here, the dream
within the rock

awakening
(myself crystal
inclusion, lens
to concentrate
this place). Place hands
on water, stream caressing

mutually, sing
praise, shout out loud
to mountain,
voicing lasting
momentary
rush off highest

cloud & peak, drink
deep the mountainous
surge, channel
divinity &

wrestle down
angelic choir

here converged. Salt
shock of jerky
opens lips to speak
spirit of mountain
now in me
made flesh. Refreshed

my muscles stream
upstream again.

Mo's Song
(how vultures sculpt)

How vultures sculpt the silence, as if
air were mountain to be carved by
feathers, endlessly. Hold quill to this.
Scratch against huge emptiness your
swoops and spiralings, your cosmic dance
to no known music. Be what majesty
teeters on outstretched wings, always
recovering, to lift life skyward and
to ground recurrent heaven here—
bring down to breathless earth rebirth.

June's Sonnet
(rising)

Come ocean wind far inland, stirring
leaves. Come weave your currents into trees.
Come make the mountains breathe, as cradles
rocking endlessly to surge of sea.
So let me see this clearly ever—
as mountain air, wind-scoured, as granite
landscape scored & polished to high song.
Let me be this vessel continent
caressed by planet's swell and pulse, on
molten seas hard tossed, earth's spiral touch
re-sculpting every peak & crevice
each breath I take, each moment here. So
let my life be always rising, always
softly seaward then subsiding.

Vince's Song
(basics)

We're back to basics, deep knee
bend in woods, legs tight in their
hard memories of off-trail hard
terrain. Stand up to pain of body
strengthening, as warmth of sun
up over mountain reaches me
relaxing into day, moist smell
of humus rising to sun's touch.

Back home, think all the things
to learn again: Warm fingers
the reward for doing dishes.
Warm cotton tee-shirt fitting like
warm day. Warm summer walk
to grocery, everything you need
right there. Warm taste of red
tomato from back garden eaten
apple-like (the way my uncle
did). Warm feel of rounded acorn
squash at farmers market (sampling
to find right one) then smiles
all round from woman there
exchanging coins, warm-pocketed.
Warm muscles chopping wood all fall
to warm ourselves another year.

It comes back down to harvest.
Up here in touch how every bite
grows ripe with thankfulness.
Sweet water washes off the sweat.
And every taste, I'm saying grace.

Marta's Reverie
(into stone)

She dries herself
and starts
          to read, then
leans back into
stone,
          eyes closed,
                    clothed
only in
soft sunlight
          filtering
through trees

to touch her
everywhere,
          breeze ruffling
& rearranging warmth
on skin
          she
also touches
          light
                    as light
at curvature

of breast,
          then lets
                    go into
dream
her body singing with

all things.

June's Song
(song)

Song twining
up whole mountain
as I climb—

each bird here
its own
bright feathered air—

twining
one around
another

to out sing
new song—
as lovers

twine
their long
melodic

lines—
twining star-ward
into time—

twining solos
met by rhyme.

6

• • •
• •

Friday

June's journal: *Mo's missing*

One a.m. Done writing. Drifting off
towards dream, all hell breaks loose, head count one
down—Mo's missing. Everyone explodes
into the night, shouts, searchlights needling
sea-urchin-like. Dave says, 'Only way
we find him is he wants us to.' I say
he said he'd found an altar stone up
top divide of these two streams. We swarm
the mountainside like flies to carcass
buzzing mad. He's stretched out quiet as
stars stabbing down into wide open
eyes, his body shivering cold
resonance of stone and sky.
                              We take
him down, wrap jackets tightly round him,
bundle back to camp. No good. Can't speak,
the hypothermia so deep his
core stone cold. Ok, I say, I know
the protocol (no guy here up to it).
I take him in, cocooned within one
mummy bag, transfusing him my heat
or else he dies.
                 Long time we lie, his
stillness terrifying, my hands upon
him like stone sculpture, numbing so

I take them back, rub rapidly
together like to make a fire or
a prayer, then lay hands on again, full
now & ladling to him what warmth
we can sustain between us. Body
pressed full-length along his back, my breasts
involuntarily erect (feeling
welling through me: to nurse the earth
starts here with us), round growing warmth now
starts to flow—long, slow return—feeling
here capillary action heating up
my hands too at their task—how stunningly
equipped, I think, we are for this, for
keeping self
                    circulating through each
other, through wide earth, sun holding us.
Then, seismically, the shaking starts, deep
up from both of us the tremors as
in death throes or at birth, we cannot
know, just trust, what's happening here—must.
No warning, suddenly my hand hits
hard into his chest, then quickly pulls
away as if dam bursting from him
torrenting hot tears. He cries and cries
all over me like I have never seen
how many tears a man can hold.
Then trembling with him, I kiss salt
from his face, say, it's ok, go on,
go on, long as you want.
                              Odysseus,
I smile then to myself, near dead from
surging ocean waves, no crew, no raft,
no clothes there at the end, after long
dream, rises from humus, gentling
so not to frighten adolescent
girls out doing laundry streamside in
the routine morning sun.
                              So here I am,
strange man in hand, long night near dawn, and

wanting only to hear how he has
come back again.
     I'm fingering one
strand of leather at his chest, strung through
black scarab (only stitch left on) when
he first says, 'So from now on I'm here
because you're here.' Black amulet, black
night rolled into it, now shines & shimmers
with first touch of sun—my touch on him—light's
glistening progeny now spreading
everywhere our warmth.

       All day in sunny
aspen grove we talk, leaves chattering
above, life stories interwoven
easily as stream flows next to us
down valley.
     Strangest thing, he can't stop
talking now—and I can't seem to get
enough of it. I'm there with him now free
to say what I could not imagine
yesterday. Seems both of us know now
what we're about. 'That was the end of it
for me,' he says. 'I see so clearly
how I can't go back to how it's been—
must open up
     new practice giving
voice to all of this, accounting for
whole picture (need app to metrically
keep count of carbon content of each
vote on every measure, then amass
per member so
     we know the weight
of our each vote back home—in aggregate
with our own measures taken there,
constituent responsibilities
like footprints
     tracked).' Then slowly adds, 'We shall
account ourselves bonded

              in covenant
of this one planet.' So on, all day
we trade as if shared futures, finally
redeemed to dream again—the way
slow currency
              of stream through meadow
will meander, sensuous &
serpentine back in on self to build
its rich deposits there beside us.
Late light, we're watching
              fish surfacing
to kiss slow flexing skin of water
holding sky—as worlds long separate
momentarily meet—round ripples spreading
out, and down through depth, and up, soft sounds
rounding the evening's pliant air.

Sixth fire: *Life*

Life , having learned to turn its toxins
into resource generating
heightened

2.4 BYA - *aerobic*
respiration
                        energy , spins forth burning
with renewed potential , sunlight folded
into carbon , blazing back at touch
of oxygen ,
              elaborating
twenty times more potent & intense
than fermentation
                        previously
had stewed , in its long drawn out stupor.

Aerobic partnering

That energy recurrently
pent & spent
              quickly fuels increasingly
diversifying forms of life :

amoeboid
       anaerobic *cyano-*
bacteria first partnered with
aerobic
       cells , equipped to off-load
oxygen : as from a ship ,
           heavy
with hazardous material
longshoremen , once in energetic
droves , finessed
         safely ashore : till next
(inherent in amoeboid tendencies)
said transfer automates , engulfing
out-sourced labor , and
         once brought on-board
those aerobes specialize : becoming
mitochondria within host cells ,
scrubbing
       up oxygen , to stoke new-
fangled furnaces :
        alternatively ,
motoring pre-mitochondrial
aerobic cells
       speedboat out across wide
oceans , bows erect , sucking up fresh air
in their newfound acceleration
then , corkscrew , into
        vintage cells
harboring photosynthetic
chloroplasts : & find it
        advantageous
to adapt
     to mutual benefit :
spark-plugging thus new universe
of life , such
       puttering (as in garage
teenagers soup-up engines , moving on
to music , maybe , silicon :

invention driving
                    information
then : in reverse , new data looping
back , intensifying drives) hard drives us
up , crazy , round
                    round moon
                              and back again.

Nuclei arise

So life strikes up among its various
strategies , alliances
                    that given
time , combine , one cell derived from
several : so
                    seeded , oxygen-inspired
mitochondria grow armies , mopping
up O atoms inside every cell :
so in
          aerated frenzy , rank
                              ranks
swell
          like sorcerer's apprentices
to symphony , desperately
                              in need
of orchestration : stirred
                              in response ,
long chords
                    of larval DNA , long
twisting , randomly , through
                              watery
cells (and drifting , too , mitotically , one
cell to next , out
                    through space , down time ,
carrying , itinerant architects ,
templates
                    of proteins first impressed ,
inspired , at first solitary
start of life , perfecting

ever since) now
coalesce to nucleus : raise up
baton
with single touch to move
all parts : to metamorphose : to one
harmony & purpose.

2.0 BYA,
*eukaryotic
cells evolve*

Earth's memory

Information
replicated & transmitted , written
down in dyad code
passed round & down
2 billion years of life experience
adjusted , time to time , to match new
facts & happenstance—
long winding
flexible and future trending
memory of earth—
now comes to bear
one central fruit & granary at core
of each new cell
to guide now ever
more & more complex new enterprise
of integrated life : as long
strewn lines
of words , out-reaching their near endless
combinations , here
compress themselves
to page : turn book-like : then collect as
central library accessible
to all : arcane
perhaps as phone
directories from every city
siloed inside single pillared pile :
yet
holding forth , Rosetta-like (or
as old Ma Bell operator at her
motherboard hand held
amazingly) small

101

universal
            ciphers for all
parties to connect.

Dragons within

            Uncanny stillness
permeates the air, as if forest
were breathing.
                  Fire spirals fluidly
unwinding dragon coils in constant
metamorphosis responsive to
dark conjuring.

                  Still steadily descends
slow snow of death , accumulating
down cold ocean depths : as ashen
fallout from
                  necropolis of burning
libraries (& every institution
held therein) : as life's long processes
inevitably
                  break down , wear thin
defining
                  membranes , to release
                              remains
to the abyss : in preparation
for which , ceaseless life so spreads and
multiplies , each
                  cell (and every cell
in aggregate) sparks small and brief , and yet
lights up eternity : as stars : or
fireflies
                  on summer nights (prolific
as first touch
                  once first in love) flick on &
off : self scattering
                  to selfless dark
where other life re-gathers
                        and re-sparks :

so through such process , every life outlives
itself to seed life's processes
through seas ,

through time , through churning change , breaking
all boundaries : as still within
tight
labyrinth intestine , life takes life ,
breaks
bread , spills : red , fermented wine
(free flowing deep intoxicant)
transfiguring
all offerings
in death
to live again.

I'm thinking fire
simmering (Velociraptor nest)
sighs forth first fire
breath (T. rex &
Allosaurus precedents) as death
embodied
rises up, flares into life
fierce-fanged, devouring.

So then , sun , sealed
in chloroplastic cells : attracts
attack from foraging aerobes
disinterested
in settling : intent
to ravage energy to the last
drop & then : move on : predation's born
of surplus sugar
icings , enticing
flame tongues to taste , to feed sharp appetite
of respiration (dragon taken
in , now re-released to feed
itself

1.0 BYA -
heterotrophy
arises

in feeding on itself) : life's new found
fires burning bright on pyres lit with living
sacrifice.

Warring intelligence

         To which life , marshaling
all sides , devises & deploys
immense array of counter forces
grappling not just with
                    environment
but life itself redoubling back
on itself : up against death , life
driven by
           its own intensifying
force , shatters
               prismatically , new
species splintering along new paths
of capture and escape , dance and
avoidance , pirouetting
                wildly
through wide swirling seas : swirling
                       within ,
intelligence stretches flexible
long lines
           back through time to rummage all
molecular accomplishments
in search of answers
              newly relevant :
as strategists
          that black night prior to
each day's decisive confrontation
unfurl old maps & stratagems , pore
over every detail that
                might match
(or not) the current
            changing circumstance
then issue orders : taking their best
shots , 10 , 000 times re-echoing

down chain
           to each sole soldier taking
also his best aim : one-off : resounding
& recoiling instinctively
at gory glory
           long harangued by
upper ranks to fortify faint hearts :
whoever makes it through
                 reports back
that success : that information then
digested adds to mix : binary
life & death
           now keeping count at gate
of generations massing towards next
chance.

Dark energy of death

          Intensifying energy
within , life
           draws in other life to
reignite : orbits collapsing like
electrons spin & net themselves more
tight : like appetite
            of gravity
first formed of granulated stars
prolific planets , swelling , pregnant with
all possibilities : so life
               now
pulls self into self
            condensing
massively , absorbing seas of
random cellulated energy :
while death (ultimate
               unknown , knowing
no boundary , yet final limit
infinite) like
           that dark energy
pervading everything , infusing

form to galaxies : so death informs
life's purposes , to drive
                              beyond
constraint of time , vacuity of
space , to deepest
                    mystery , then back
its memories erased , its wisdom
(encapsuled in dense nucleated tomes)
enlarged & clarified : by that
                              pitched
night baptized into evolving light.

Perfected sex

Life tasting its own fruit grows most
in knowledge of itself : from
                              first kiss
of first cells , sharing
                         first impressions
flesh to flesh , to all-consuming passions
(sublimated sometimes into dance
of predator & prey) in
                       mutual
oscillation , cat &
                    mouse , in play
in hiding , in & out , even unto
death
        escaping to bound back : restraint
& excess twined : so in
                         hopscotching
sacrifice , life dances cross (old school-
yard) blacktop , chalking up hard numbered days
to necessary
              learning : till , in
sweet time , pigtails give way to combing
longing adolescent waves mirroring
self
        facing self : and in such knowing
on through eons of nucleic life

& death improvisations , acid tests :
life so perfects
        self-replication
(folding innovations in for next
new cell split off from parent) finally
we hit on
        sex : 2 parents sharing
split of imaged replicates re-spliced
to knit new individual
holding twice
        the knowledge , or more
accurately , the possibilities
to shape itself to spin (turn-tabling
roulette) from scratch
        to hit best odds , best
combinations for success in changing
world : and more : most opportunity
to mismatch steps
        along long helix
generating novelty unthought
before (or else disaster) : or for
best chance of chance
        mutation flecked
by ultraviolet photon strobing
planetary membrane , maybe , or
environmental
        stimulant at
large on spinning earth.

1.0 BYA -
sexuality
arises

Dragons calmed

        Coals pulsing like
sunlight on water—we watch together
steady warmth rise up in us, wash
over, inundate, impart
        one song
now we know by heart.

        Now the music
sweetens and again accelerates

to mutual beat of new attraction
drumming up
        new chemistries among
still-single cells ping-ponging &
triangulating
        food & fear & sex
to keep one step ahead , keep in
the mix : in time
        things settle into
dancing thus : hip-hoppy , though still
flowing , too , through each new
        generation
(scratch that
        go back , start over
        try again)
continuous : as here this
        fire dying
down , still feeds the dragons it contains :
sensuous as water , coiling
sharp-spined
        through flame : such dragon as we've
read lays down embattled head upon
a woman's lap , who
        tentatively
strokes that smoldering massif , and musing
on it , Pele-like , smoothes out rough
adamant to black
        sand beach her white
hands calm , caress, the way calmed sea laps
at new land , its chimneyed contours
rounding
        smooth as page of book , breaking
wave-like in toward spine : her
        hand there
toying every word , jet letter (alpha
to omega) , whole sensed syntax of
illuminated
        tome of life , she
turns to open & spread wide next page—

yielding up her body to such stuff
as dreams
   reconstitute to be
soft touch of cosmos
     into her as
flowing nebulae harden to trillion
gamete stars , each harboring unique
bright futures to unwind
     and in her
silk imaginings , silk streaming
passages
   to new dreams
     recombine :

1611 – Shakespeare,
'The Tempest'

those white foam hands so soothe those hardened
battlements , restoring all to peace ,
all heroes & their dragons :
     all fears
and pleasures rounding out all pages of
all books , knowledge continuous : as
if hard words
    turn liquid , sensitive
to touch : as cloud
     drifts off , becoming what
we want of it : so death , so life , so love
dream us and all our passages.

Colonies unite

*He takes round branch of proper radius
& length & works it into fire
teasingly to stir*
    fresh radiance
outpouring to us.

    As log on log
rightly arranged , sustains
     long mutual

flame : some cells
already urbanized
(dense colonies glommed onto under-
water rock to share resources and
security : round-domed
long bubbling
stromatolites : or algae strung-out
streaming into kelp) now further
specialize
spurred on by growing
intimacy evolving in response
to need and outreach of close neighbor
cells : so some become
protectors
communicators or digesters : all
roles rolled up in spiraling dance of
genes , to pass on
cumulative

1.2 BYA -
*multicellular
organisms
evolve*

sufficient
knowledge : not just to run
one cell , but multiplex collective
organism : now nucleic
core of every cell
holds knowledge of
the whole : and also that deep wisdom
to hold back , direct , expression
of such vast potential
to : specific
time & place : so each succeeding cell
unfurls in harmony with larger
purpose.

We have such knowledge in us

So knowledgeable , now rounding
out from single cell (combining
double imprint of its parents) blooms
embryonic sphere

of cells (all potent
with whole history & future of
whole planet) growing
steadily toward
sovereign self of differentiated
parts : globed *blastula* : like sunrise out
of ocean , scattering
new life : as
light first burst through universe and then
again , incalculably : as starbursts
scored & scripted
differentiated
elements , each with specific
energies.

He stares up into sky
receiving dome of heaven down
into his eyes, the fire bedded
down like stars
still warming us.

We have such
knowledge in us of our sources
and intents : we carry this deep sense
in every cell now knowing
what it means
to be all things : connected cosmically
at root and in potential : yet
the sense as well
to choose to flower
individually : to touch and reach
and serve
unfolding worlds you hold within
and feel around you everywhere :
round planet now grown self-aware.

Jose's Lament
(the accident)

He'd reached that time he
only wanted to sit back
and watch the maples grow.
He'd started out wanting to be
in forestry, off in his tower
somewhere like an Ent, reading
all day between brief scans
of the horizon looking out for
fire — judging which clouds
might thunder & ignite whole
forest, which ones were actual
smoke, which ones bore deliverance
of water deep to root. All this
he knew by heart, just starting
out, but had to quit to get real
work, look out for those like me
he loved — or Mom, just taking it
all in. She knew his sacrifice,
that that was how things were.
But now he'd get his chance
to go 'grow leaves' he said, go
watch the woods each autumn
(late shift of sun's kaleidoscope)
dance into air, then settle down
to gladly darken earth again.
And watch his kids and mine
grow old in time. Economy
then forced him back to work —
'Lucky they'll still have me.'
Sawmill took him in. Then
spit him out the other end.

He hung on through those dying
days. 'Must know your limits,'
he would say. In & out of dream
he seemed that way to staunch
the pain — then finally let go

the flow back out of him, as river
at the mouth of ocean knows
the tides now measure
what we once thought ours.

Vince's Song
(which war?)

Which war is this?
My soul's lost track.
So many maimed
and dead ideas we
still fight on, fight
for. Which war?

Do not answer
easily. The dead
want none of that.
They know what's
said is all we have
to rest on in the end.

Answer to them.

Meru's Song
(gold mtn.)

Go east
my man
to dawn
gold egg

(&cestors
say).

Go
scramble
up gold mtn.
cook, consume,
dig in, sluice out,
extract, melt
down, remint
round disc.
Shine
it.

Go
interview
(shine shoe?)
Go NYU.
Go climb
gold mtn.
Go
(got dime?)

Here us:
c cirrus
wisp wan
dragon's
breath
extinct
extinguished
gone

expended.
Old mtn. now
no more
defended.
Go

join
up.
Go gun. Go
take
last
rights.

Gold bullets
make
& shrapnel all
of this.

Gold sunrise
but replenishes.

Lily's Song
(what kind of world)

We just were
wild. I lost
the father, then
the child. I ask
myself, what kind
of world would that
have been for
her? Not wanting
much to know.
So now, for me
it's all about
my lesson plan—
everything &
anything beyond
that made-up
world I came from,
world of real make
believe. Can't
hardly breathe
so much hot air, such
stuff we got
from everyone
just trying to be
cool, be doing
their own thing—
on dollars, dope
or preaching
opiate
as antidote.
Who would have thought
out here
this wildness
gentles out to touch
& holds so much? Now
my own arms
around
myself, like mountain
strong,

I'm working on
the world
to get it ready for
my girl, whenever
I might feel our
time turn ripe
again—at least
enough this time
to play for keeps.

June's Song
(owl speaks)

Owl speaks to me
familiar calling,
'Who, who—who?'

Dream-like all night
far answerings fly in.
Then dawn, they're gone.

But now I know,
god-like, guidance
lives here. I wander

with her everywhere.

Mom's Psalm for Me
(June)

I am
your ocean. You be
also the sea, long
swelling generations
after me. Be

wave enveloping
steep shore—be
waves on waves
voluptuously
surmounting every
height.

Be moonlight
swimming
in its millions in
earth's wake across
surface of night.

Dazzle
your pure
promise bright
as sequins
slipping
from bare skin.

Teem wet within
with seed
of forests yet

to be.
Ave Maria be. *Ave.*
Ave. Bowed wings as
angel, white as
wave, raise
up

your voice
all ways
in praise.

Mo's Well Dream
(sweet & deep)

There was a baby once
thrown down a well
but rushes buoyed him
from drowning. In time
child weaves them
into basket floating
there in total blackness.
Looking up far telescoping
shaft, he sees a star, far
speck of hope fading
away to dove-gray
dawn, dove call
resounding down
to him. Then slowly vision
shifts to one blue disc,
cloud-swirled & marbled,
hovering long days upon
deep dark till nights again
close in. Mosquitoes then
materialize to
puncture infant
skin. He says to them,
'Inoculate me from
whatever breeds here
I'm not meant for.' Rats come
scrounging, and again he says,
'Come close and lick
this blood from me so that
your sharp saliva kills
all pestilence. Come
soothe raw wounds.' Then from
those deepest waters no one
knows, long serpents
needle-fanged arise, bright
piercing eyes enquiring.
He answers them, 'What would
you do?' They pause,
discussing, then begin
weaving themselves

together, reaching up slow
twisting flames into the dark,
shedding old skins
like silver smoke they braid
into long rope
to tie umbilically
to that high sky now turning
gold & silver dawn
again, then floating
azure dome. Up reaching
tender fingers
child unleashes scream
of such deep
longing it reverberates
upwelling over all
the town all day, all night
a month & ten
nights counting, the
citizens afraid
to sleep, their dreams
so haunted with
remembrance
of long abandoned
well, thought dry
or polluted, clearly
now demented
spirit's lair. None dare
approach for fear
of it. Until one girl
one morning hears
in her own heart
deep cry re-echoing
and walks out there
alone, takes hold
of rusted gears & turns
well winch till silver
snakeskin cord brings up
wet dripping basket
from which steps a child
exactly her age. His eyes
grow round embracing round
horizon then return

to her soft smile,
her hand outstretched
to him. They walk then
hand in hand, returning
into wide-eyed town,
from that day on
administering
all people there
their dreams, drawn from
those desert waters
sweet & deep.

Mo & *June's* Duet
(forever blossoming)

I love to feel you deep inside.

I love to feel you deep inside
me surge like ocean, rise like stem.

We surge like ocean, rise like stem
that pulls the earth up into leaf.

That leafs & roots & flowers me throughout
as stars give galaxies their birth.

That roots & leafs & flowers me throughout
black night that doesn't end.

Deep night forever blossoming.

Mo's Love Song
(for June)

Time's this
anomaly
that we
create.

Deadlines,
we call them,
finish lines.
Make haste.

But when we met
the nameless
(wondering
could this be it?)

and death
shone through
like white
of our own

skulls, come
finally
face to face,
in us

we saw
the power
then to bend
an hour into

everything
we want—
the way
the universe

wants us
to stop, then
pull out all
the stops

and play
as if
the endless
music

ends today.

Mo & *June's* Duet
(streamside)

'I am touched by, and here I touch
the universe in you, its curvature
towards us—smooth rising contour of your
hip, long waves of hair my fingers brush,
slow currents combing through our depths.'

'I intertwine my length with yours, our
limbs encoiled & ingrained as tree
trunks meant from birth to share one place under
the sun—and flow & blaze together
here our years, as tree rings consummate

sand earth & grainy stars in marriage.'

Mo & June's Duet
(one child)

We want the one
of sun, of moon—
one earth in orbit
all encompassing

dancing among
as child in spring
around us ever
mother, father

everything, one
child to heal
and care for,
one spirit with us

inner, outer—
one as all
and one as only
one can know,

one song and one
creation sings,
creation carrying
we two as one—

as child, *as song*
to carry on—
as love, our love
at every turn.

7

. .
. . .
. .

Saturday

Seventh fire: *Gaia*

Gone multicellular, life mushrooms,
swims and blossoms
                    open ; radiating
myriad forms (each innumerable
millions strong) ; spreading bright rays & fins
& fingers out
            to sculpt round earth's
fecundity set free
                    again to reach
and relish untold possibilities ;
from sex-fused
                blastula (hot-wired
with experience, packing dense
bulge
        of energy) explodes now
detonating speciation
overtaking
                far pre-Cambrian
horizons like tsunami from one
triggering eruption inundating
everything ; so life

                        begins ascent
up scales, upsizing
                    to commodious

extent of planet ; building, cell on
cell, soft tissues issuing all shape
and manner of expression, every
pattern latent
               in them and all their
combinations ; all again to mold
themselves to fit responsively
the pressures of wide world forever
pulsing out beyond.

Life globular

                    Grown globular,
ballooning life pumps oceans through it
filtering
              nutrients (consuming
life less corpulent) & pumping, too,
itself ; to push self unabashedly
forward through syruped seas,
                        consumption
inextricably entrained in sweet
mobility ; like planets
                riding
pastured seas of light, life pulses,
sometimes trailing back
                    long arms the better
to embrace escaping sustenance ;
or comb-like, wave-like, like
                  aurora
borealis shimmering bright tresses
to advance
         soft
             irresistible
designs, life shimmies side to side ; or as
anemone, inverted, upside-
down, gone stationary, planted,
flowering
             slow fingers out to feel
(with sharp pang) each particle of life
adrift, in currents rippling as

600 MYA -
jellyfish &
other soft
organisms

126

flesh of ocean opens its deep lap
& yielding
            curvatures : life grasps
whatever passes for its own
expansive purposes.

Spiral shells molluscular

                        As under-
water net of light, or canopy
of leaves, bright fire here aspires back
as if transcendent trees.

                        Drawing on
long line of DNA-encrypted
memory how best to grapple out
from saturated seas pure mineral
extract (gold, for
                instance, panned from stream
by settler bacteria, turned ore
to vest in vaulted earth for future
generations ; or carbonates
of silica or
            calcium, like
snowflakes, crystallized at core of single-
celled progenitors, to drop like stars
in drifts accumulating over
ocean floor) life
                aggregating its
capacities, swirls outward spiral
shells, molluscular, as strong-armed storms
or galaxies , grown large enough far
future eyes might
                plainly see (embedded
in hard stone) Cambrian explosion
of proliferating forms like
shrapnel
            ripping up (from depth of earth)
all previous perceptions of
earth's birth ; as we now Hubble back through

550 MYA -
'Cambrian
explosion' of
shells &
arthropods

127

time to find first aggregated
nebulae expanding
                        out to reach
us (in wide wonder) from
                                    first touch of
radiant creation.

Core need to know
                        Life hardens,
hunkers down within rock walls against
rapacious ocean of free moving
life, all circling, softly cylindrical,
one end
            to take food in
                                then, aft, excrete,
everything between digestion ; but
for core need to know
                        what to do
next ; each part & every cell in concert
with the rest (first from round blastula
to differentiate ; then to
coordinate ; then finally shape
                                    response
to outside stimulus) ; especially
those most mobile creatures ; freely
plumbing fluid depths to orient
within
            that ambient matrix of
subsistence, threat, and always churning
love ; need now sure knowledge & cohesion
to inform themselves (so deeply
malleable) so as
                    deeply to delve
new sifting universe they navigate.

Accordingly, upwelling chemistries
wash over every cell like waves
of music bathing
                    all in harmonies

we rise to, held in sway by these
new seas
                    surging within ; life
                                    channeling
molecular communications
shapes conduits (as mail chutes from old
high-proofed, deadline-driven newsrooms rush
copy to print) lined with
                                    articulate
cilia to speed said process (key
strokes singing in unison) themselves
becoming (next edition could be) pulse
transmitting
                    coded information ;
then fashions neurons
                                lengthening
electric axis parallel to
alimentary canal ; synapses
snapping with bright energy of stars
to sharpen
                    life's emergent imagery
of what, when, who, how, where.

Wormholes conduct

                                    Ancestral
to our own line, primordial worms (worm-
holes of which conduct us still through
Cambrian slate) first circle pinging   525 MYA -
spinal chords   *vertebrates*
                    protectively with
cartilage ; leveraged then to skeleton
soon strung with lengthening musculature
connecting out to sculpt whole body
into motion
                    matching shark-like sweep
& surge of ocean
                            that new vertebrates
soon rule.

He stops & sits bolt upright
lengthening like Puritan in
wooden pew, or Buddhist in deep state
of meditation, while all around
our circle
    muscles tighten down on
bone involuntarily—then in long
exhalation soften.

Think that hard
structure mined from earth, mineral
precipitate of stars, no longer
bunkered round fail-safe, but taken in
to structure you
    to new
        fluidity
of action ; we're built from centered spine
& discipline of knowing ; flowing
in, then amplified back out
        through every
rhythmic act that constitutes connected
reach of life.

    Feel scepter bone move up
your back, each segment testament to
flex of notochord through ocean
sediment ; tough
    cartilage of shark
still padding every joint ; shark jaw &
teeth still rising silent rush up dark
bone corridor, consuming you in
flood of fear
    each unaccounted sound
crouched cougar night
      might make ; listen and
glory in undifferentiated
knowledge deep within ; as embryo
experiences in darkness mother's

heartbeat and, in
                    sea of womb, tries on
vestments & vestiges of its own
evolution ; piecing together,
sorting out, all possibilities, in
time, one comes
                    to term ; choosing unique
cohesions & expressions ; weaving
in perhaps new trends
                    or random
flourishes ; while patterning always
enduring themes we all still wear ; cut
from same cloth, woven together on
same looms.

Free swim
                    Life now circumnavigates
all coasts, heads upstream from ocean,
testing rich reach of its inhabited
inheritance ; free swimming
                    fish hold
sway in
                    currents (alternating side
to side) of their own making
                    making
headway, neuronal pulse of spine
imparted through bright pulse of water ;
brain
          articulated foremost
                    finely
balances in steady mastery
one moment, next
                    one flashes quick
crescendo ; like rest of body now
finessed, in touch with self & place ;
synapses
          coalesce ; discuss among
themselves ; work out
                    next steps ; exquisitely

520 MYA - *fish*

131

as pectoral fins softly modulate
positions
      fore & aft ; ascent &
descent (with assist
        perhaps from sacs
recycling waste CO_2 to
lift & bolster buoyancy) ; or as
lip-syncing guppies gulp
       & then
          release
(as in
   old silent movie
      bellowing)
each breath ; enunciating perfectly
one small globe rising
     up
      from sea.

Highrise skedaddle

While over ocean floor skedaddle
tank-like arthropods
     on tensile legs
(as if equipped for gravity on
moon or mars) ; and algal
     seaweeds, long
strung-out, washed up incessantly on
desiccating shores (left there, twice
daily tidal sacrifice to sun)
find life prolonged
     by fashioning walled
cells of celluloid (sea water
reservoirs) that stacked up end on end
high-rise

450 MYA -
*plants go
ashore*

   green chlorophyll into blue sky ;
first plants, first organisms on dry
land ; then likewise
     armored tight against
bright arid air, crustaceans belly up

to greener pastures ; harboring inside
hard shell, sea's softness curled ; themselves
small footstep ponds
                        of ocean hurrying
in waves ashore.

To weave the wind
                        First flattened in
unmitigated gravity,
in time
            insects & spindle-legged
arachnids rise teetering into
thin air at brink
                        of land ; downsizing
self to dance lightly in step, attuned,
to earth's specific
                        mass ; next even
stepping off
                        from plant tops ; parachuting
out pure self-spun silk or tissued wings
to float aloft on air ; to circle
swirling atmosphere ; to weave the wind,
high cirrus lines
                        encompassing
whole planet ; while in

                        slow concert, plants
continue pushing higher through warm air
(jointed, equisetum-like) their
structures hardening
                        to hold moisture
within ; while spreading out branched, paneled
solar surfaces open to sun
like hands raised up
                        in celebration
welcoming sky down, in intimate
embrace of earth ; from which, prolific
populations likewise push & spread

420 MYA - *insects*

up branching
streams imprinted by wet touch
of rain, patterning
the land, plant-like ;
till sexuality ; as yet constrained
to mud banks, pools, smooth rounding reach
of rivers (where plant gametes release
themselves
back into eddying wet
possibility) ; now consummates
in trees grown ever more erect ; perfects
first seeds (droplets aswim within thin
sac) releasing

390 BYA – *conifers,*
seeds encased

life to stitch green-needled
canopies, thick-cuticled across
whole continents
wherever wind
will carry and rain germinate.

Life carboniferous

Thus carboniferous
life spreads its
mantle over earth's own mantle, owning

360 MYA -
Carboniferous
period

it afresh ; grown geologic in
extent & depth ; luxuriant first
terrestrial paradise
patrolled by
multifaceted kaleidoscopic
consciousness
of dragonflies dividing
up lush air (their fractal eyes reprising
understory fern) ; green darner stitches
self down into serendipitous dark
vein of carbon ; one
still moment
captured & entombed ; & with it, whole
still swamp turns inward ; anaerobic ;
pressed to peat ; then over-layered by sands

of seas
            rising periodically
as glaciers melt ; rich
                    sediment
of rising mountains washing down
& back inland again to churn &
curl of continents ; beside lush seas
lush forests
            rise, subside, wide midlands
(first submerged in ocean) giving ground
to oceanic trees ; thus forest
(Gaia-goddess-like) and sea (rotund
as Aphrodite) breathe
                    in & out
long rhythmic oscillations (gold sands
to bluest depths to deep green shade) ; every
breath
            of starburst *diatom* or *cycad*
reconstituting atmospheric
carbon
            into life ; by which
                            life
infinitesimally adjusts
earth's thermostat
                    to cool or warm
to suit recurrent needs ; overriding
even asteroid or volcanic
                    storms.

Carbon futures
                            Limbs
streaming up through air veined traceries
(as vaulted choirs
                    hold high-pitched stained glass)
to meet down-streaming light, convert
sun's energy to life life saves (in
death) against hard time : carbon futures
safe-deposited
            within rich earth

(as diamond rings might be) ; also sea's
endless caress
                    of solar shafts (gold
& silver disked into her furrows) sifts
coccolithophoriditic
algal cysts
                    of carbonate out from
solution : limed precipitate
that structures floating photosynthesis
then spiraling, snow-like, precipitates
itself to drifts
                    of limestone ; woven ;
pressed ; inclined sometimes
                                        to catch last pure
black concentrate of life, held liquid
in inverted
                    chalice someday raised
to unborn acolyte : thus life
expansively responds to carbon
freshly washed from mountains ; belched volcanically
to air (or expired there
by its own
                    respiration) ; growing
prodigiously intensified
by growing heat held close to earth by
hothouse CO_2 ; till luminous
algae blooms
                    dimethylsulfide
seeding air to blossoming high clouds
that cool things down ; rain
                                        down upon fresh
forests ; which, with oceanic algae
reabsorb rank carbon (as also
annual snows compose seawater into
towering
                    white ice caps & mountain
glacial floes) ; storing and transfiguring
carbon again to soil, oil, coal & stone :
earth's climate, too, re-steadied and reset

by life's cyclic
                 & cumulative
florescence.

Small gardens

        Thinking how forests flare
back into life once flame has blackened
them—curling chartreuse against dead coals
as life in conflagration fuels new
life, sparks
           pouring up to milky
galaxy fresh stars to punctuate
ink skies.

       Today perhaps you followed
fir & spruce up tight granitic
drainages to find small gardens
nestled close to stem of stream, like clustered
fruit : compacted
           Paradisos,
poised *Ryoanjis* perfectly composed
of random parts ; pure sunlight passing
through warm petaled flesh of lily, oranged
by it ; or purple
           shooting stars flared
back in readiness to penetrate
smooth
       flow of water under them, each set
as gem against gray granular dissolve
of granite textured with stray mica
touch of parent star ; or air alive
with insects, wild
           bumbling array
infused with scent & color, all
scrambled & admixed in honeyed
partnership of sex : what gardens are
prepared
       for us, what Edens here invite
our care & tending to, once made aware.

130 MYA - *flowers*

Earth marbled

Look further then, up past last fir to
stone austerity majestically
enticing you
        higher ; not so far
removed from what faced life's first faceted
ascent ; fresh igneous uplift
scraped clear by glacier (still each winter
wearing its
        white remnants) ; spring-scoured
year on year ; even so (both now and then)
no blank canvases confront us, but
(look again) bright
        splattering of lichens ;
every pigment (Pollock-like) blottered
on boulders ; luminance of algae
riding back of symbiotic
fungus
        solid-footed up & over
every rock ; enzymes sunk like teeth
cramponed on living stone, digesting
minerals to nourish blooming sheens
of photosynthesis ;
        the way
mycelia (but one cell thick
to keep exquisitely in touch with
earth) likewise become foundational
to forests
        spreading miles above one
all-connecting organism ; think
deep down within earth's mantle teeming
nearly infinite bacteria ;
gleaning ;
        percolating ; cooking up
vast chemistry of planet ; earth rendered
to one life comprised of all lives ; earth
marbled

through with life ; round garden
tending to itself, round-circuited
to tip excesses into balance ;
all missteps
            dissolving twig-like back
to forest floor ; to rise again high
overhead, fine traceries of limb
supporting everything ; each factory
leaf (sun-stoked, earth-fed
                    in precision
equilibrium) ; each fragrance in
each breath knit through
                    with chemistries each
species weaves to pattern self within
life's lasting fabric.

So holds the whole
                    As first yarn-balled
organic molecules began first
parsing & elaborating earth's
elemental
            composition
(dust to life and life to dust again) ;
and as evolved
            bacteria then
painted ores through rock ; and burnished air
with oxygen : so now such processes
continue to adjust within globed
blastulas (and their
                    outpouring
progeny) encompassing whole planet,
ratcheting accounts
                    of elements
in circulation globally to best
advantage of
            on-going life ; so
oxygen's held steady, rich enough
to stoke life's respiration, not so much
as sparks spontaneous

combustion ;
so atmospheric blanketing
of carbon, symbiotic with deep
breathing seas & forests, keeps

earth

at temperatures conducive to
recurrent dream of life ; so Gaian
planet learns

responsiveness to its

own being, every part

now pulsing

heart of living sphere : as every
organism holds itself in balance
with the rest, so holds the whole in deft
& intricate

unfolding dance, all

parts in motion and yet

centering

harmonically in multitudinous
repeating & reactive steps ; as
singularity of planet holds
all life secure & warm

in its embrace ;

as sun holds earth ; as galaxy beyond
spins every speck of star into long
flowing strand, woven in turn within
whole cosmos flowering

from first dark seed

of light.

Metamorphosis

Then kneel, returning now
again to that same garden font ; crouch
down and look into slow mirroring
liquid flowing stone, pure flexing flesh-like
water (maybe then

touch lips to it

to drink) ; feel grain & warmth of sand
your body leans against, noticing

perhaps gelatinous galactic
mass of eggs ; then
                        sperm-like, tadpoles in
weightless wait
                of metamorphosis ;
frog also
             noses up for air, afloat
in liquid ambiance, long legs spread wide
in lax abandon ; another
crouches wet at
                streamside bundled
fetally ; bug-eyed (as you once crouched
once out of your round ocean) readying
to spring ; cells coiled with moist memories of
such moment
                moving still through us
each breath ; each wide-webbed leap we take ;

imagine next, those first amphibious
vertebrates push up on ancient shore
granular with granite
                                                                    360 MYA -
                breasting   *amphibians*
treacherous paradise to broach new   *go ashore*
heights : first lungs (evolved from air sac
modulating fish ascendancy
and depth) now
                rising oceanic up
to inundate whole planet.

Sealing seas within
                                Fierce
fire eyes of dragonfly, sharp shards
of broken flame, frame
                                here composite
geodesic
                planet
                        taking in

(as photosynthesis did sun) now

iridescent

        knowledge winging it

zig-zag

    on thin

        transcendent heights.

              Though thus
to thrive in desiccating, sun-baked
air, first reptiles first must
            scale flesh over ;

320 MYA –
*reptiles, eggs
in shells.*

sealing seas within ; to walk dry land
far journeying away from oceans ;
drinking deep
         fresh streams to circulate
through them as they spread wide
              wide footprints
over rough terrain ; large bodied,
Rubenesque, seas sway inside them, hip
to hip (as tides ride up & down
constricted
        coasts voluminously
to mutual pull of gravities of
earth and moon in slow-paced rhythms
circling) ; so seas, swashbuckling
in thighs and bellies, also
           motion
in (as into hot, dark room midday)
emboldened full embodied sex ;
lizard libidos probing mutual
depths
      as ship prows pitch & mix, high heavy
timbered masts at sway above, among
high waves crescendoing where oceans
meet at tip
        of continent ; till ships
turn rudder ; lift (cumulous) white sails
bellying to steady winds (cargos
stowed in egg-shell calcium) ; all life's

directions
        banked within ; bound for safe
harbor ; round clutch gestating in round
mound of earth
           warm sun will incubate
& nurse each dawn ; some such
                revved up, hot
rod dragons in heat
          internalize
combustion then, steadying within
hard breathing fire.

300 MYA -
endothermy evolves

Look up

        Stand straight, look up into
tall trees to see outstretched mast-like from its
reptilian lineage
        colossal-
necked Diplodocus upraising tiny
head to strip sequoia twig ; or
(having cracked upside of gravity
with flute-like
        hollowed bone, downsizing
into flight) descendent hawk ; still gripping
scaly talons round spired pinnacle
of tree of life ; or circling sunward high
arcs clear out of sight until
        main trunk
of dinosaurs, 200,000,000
years ascendant, one day gets clear cut
(as we one day dig up) by dust of
mountain
        meteor spun off far drift
of boulders through deep space ; as here too
gravity's brought down upon these Edens
intermittent field of stone ; from which
occasionally you'll see (one
        further strand
of reptile line, egg now dispensed to warm

235 MYA -
dinosaurs

150 MYA - birds

65.5 MYA -
Chicxulub
meteor ends
Cretaceous

143

mammalian
                        womb, yolk-smooth & giving
breasts, and parents' endless
                                rounds of heart-felt
love) intelligence (that long—wormlike—
had tunneled underfoot) pop up ; slick
weasel periscoping round to see
what rubble
                        has spread out for lunch today.

June's journal: *Letter to Rich*

Seems Solstice yesterday, in fact, whole
week the longest I have ever seen—
you know how time can slow to show each
detail, stop you in your tracks to watch
things pass? Someday, if you want, when we're old

friends, I'll tell you everything I've learned—
how single word can glisten lonely
as far star, yet be galactically
connected. This is hard. You see here
teardrop (I've circled for you) smeared

on page. The truth is our long plans for
me no longer sing, the chemistry's
gone dry. Plain facts and honesty, we've
always said. For me, for now, that's it.
I'm seeing all as is. As granite.

Granite Dawn Song
(Marta)

Here's only granite—
its overburdens (like my
own) sloughed off mountain
range as snakeskin from
emergent earth—shining
again this undulant dawn.

I touch earth's curving
flesh scaled crystalline as
ice that polished it, warming
now to liquid sun. I melt
into hot all-encompassing
depths, re-hardened here

briefly round me to see.

June's Song
(dawn)

This mix
of granite,

water, gold
sun shivering

on cold
mountain

lake—on close-up
lichen, frame

of fir, far sheen
of warming

snowfields—I'll take
all day to find

my way
through it.

Marta's Song
(I kneel to see)

I kneel to see close-up a writing
spider. Is that the nomenclature,
or *garden* spider? (Think of the
communication that's transpired
in such places.) I can see now my own
breath breathe within its silk, mistaken
could it be for prey, or prayer? More
likely wind that weaves across this
mountain every detail, stirring all to
action, is it? Interaction? Life? I ask
only that my words, here woven to like
thickness as these white hieroglyphics, might
so strengthen me to catch (& be caught up
in) all that moves, all that all perceives.

Meru's Cosmology
(like web)

we each construct
like spider
web

concentric rough
facsimile
of

universe

to
catch
like mist
what most

we hunger for

Gwen's Song
(rufous hummingbird)

Ah, spark
of nectaring

intensity
come

nuzzle me
come

touch
come push

aside soft
petals

reach
deep

pollen
steep &

sweeten
me in

all your
travels:

come
home

here
& bury

us
in this

red hot
sunlit

translucence.

Jose's Song
(boxes)

Heart wood
Dad could
craft & polish
prettily to
boxes which
Mom filled
with jewels
she thought
of value.

Now I don't
know what
to do, both
gone
& me alone
& no one
caring much
about such
things.

Empty
I start to see
at heart
what's given me.

Lily's Song
*(I am experiencing
extinction)*

I am
experiencing
extinction
everyday, and not
from natural
causes but
my own.

O
I have my reasons
I don't know. Blind
as cave newt
I have adapted out
the sun, the moon
the last least
glimmering
touch
of wind—learning
bumping
headlong into
things, no, one
thing, over &
again, ungiving
prison of my own
conviction.

Let me now rise
from watery
demise

and see—
stark as tiger,
feelingly as chimpanzee,
as snake unblinkingly,
as forest full of eyes—
and know

in all those
ways the way
that I must go.

Marta's Song
(cougar)

Instinctively
I knew to stand
stone still. It seemed
to swing into
the tree, up
muscular low
branches swept
to touch hill's tawny
curvature as if
one flesh.
In round eyes like
Rousseau might
paint, the lion
held all of it
& me as in hot
dream suspended
there, liquid, intense
& yet at rest.
'The fear of God,'
I wanted then
to say. But in
his silence heard (as
if divine), 'Restraint.'
We went our separate
ways, but carry
that shared knowledge
all our days.

Vince's Dream
(cougar)

Newspaper time
I'm in my parents'
driveway when

the lion appears
among their
marigolds
to say, 'This is
my world, as well,
the one I'm
born to, down to
mean logos on
fast cars
& forests cut & squared
to shelter you. This
I accept
and mean no harm
to you, or it.

'But come with me
awhile, walk padded
through what home
remains our own.'

Mahoganies like
stone. Ginger
like red teeth marks
deep in leaf. Life
solid, all one flesh,
cut sunlight, geometric.

'*Our* own?' I ask.

'Yes, *you*
are mine,'
says lion.
'We warrior
here together.'

I follow
up steep temple
steps entwined
in vine.

There's chocolate
at the top. I drink
deep earth, her
sweetness thick, its
flavors reaching
down through
me to touch
hot heart
I'm giving freely.

It's only this
I want, warm
dawn
of forest song —
and silence
of the lion
here staring
down all fear,
protecting
worlds on worlds
to come.

'Speak steady
heart, clear mind.
Lift up just hand
rebalancing
what binds.'

Lizard's Song
(Mo)

I have not hope. I am
beyond, before. On lava
bomb, on lichen's green
& gray patina, I am speaking
here to you. Hear here. Be
parliamentary, let us.
Laws, not battle, make.

Edict: We're in this
together—lichen's gray &
green patina (all of us) of
earth, her own tenacious
speaking forth. Give voice.

Edict: Be small again
in reverence of all. Be small
with us, come down to discuss
shared ends, look up to sky
to single dream resounding
from this round rock podium
this blue transparent dome
our star all days is transiting.

Edict: Be one with sun. Go
back to earliest first aggregating
cells, their memories of all things
possible, of all dissolving into
all. Come meet me there. Stare
deep into this eye (considering
the saurian) black oculus how
many of mammalian kind once
transited. Suspend pretense
of that supreme Intelligence.
Look through my eye, burnt through
by sun, in feverish hallucination
letting loose all sense of size, each
speck on midnight sky like glint
of teeth glistening unknown

intent. Watch there one pin-prick
streak meteorically enlarge to rent
apart what meteors begot.

Take on earth's wisdom given you—
to do in your small time, small harm.

June's Song
(kinglet)

Just look
(you don't believe
what we could be)
what dinosaurs
became:

T. rex to kinglet
pirouettes
sharp-beaked
to sip midair
fine mist
of insects,
its

heart
pounding
to support same
bones first hollowed
out
to lighten frame
that shook

the earth
each step it took.

8

· · ·

· ·

· · ·

Sunday

June's journal: *Letter to Dad*

Like you—always—told me, 'decision
time' has come. So scythe in hand, I'm done
with options: Ecology's my
medicine, my service. 4 more years
@ Ithaca I'm thinking (assuming
loans still operational—or else
its 'Eco-Ec,' back to the streets, you said).
Specifically, in entomology
(as always I am wanting to pin down
each part of whole bright spectrum, blue
morpho to red admiral). Beginning
now to see the way Mom used to say,
'the weaving of the web is mostly
insects.' Here sunbeams sometimes whirling
worlds of them—like ocean streaming plankton,
or our deep gut ecologies
of anaerobes—they keep whole system
up & running. I know this isn't
what you had in mind—much riskier
and out there—but, you've kept me safe
these years to gather back my strength
and now, your warrior, I am ready
to step free and be
                    all you have fought for,
everything blossoming
                    lovely in

rich aftermath of peace, all healing
all—first tending to myself, then drawn out
in warm embrace of whole round earth
proliferating multilaterally.
I feel I am the earth now opening
to see myself, my orbit through deep
time—to see & sing this destiny
we all create through all our days.

Eighth fire: *Consciousness*

Remember early on in *Odyssey*,
Odysseus escapes those boulders tossed
from towering blind anger of
Cyclops (whom he's intoxicated,
misled, stolen blind, then run

                             a stake
through that one
                       lake-like eye, before
slipping out from rocky cave with just
as usual his wits) but turning
back to taunt, then loses (is it, two?)
ships, his own
                  come close to swamped, leaving
us wondering (too soon
                     yet to tell)
will in the end high pride defeat
heroic enterprise?

Out from under weight
                  Like that now
mammals blink at bloody sunrise
aftermath of meteor, blue
                planet
turned to dust—choked, cloaked, socked solid,
cinders settling long years through
darkness. Slowly it dawns
               on them, they

had survived, not just catastrophe
but (time down crushing out
                              of mind) high
scale-eyed, saurian conglomerate
dragon overlords here buried, left
behind as if on long
                    receding
shore, nightmare relinquishing to light
(though not without
                    recurrence). And so
surviving life's set free to contemplate
new journey. Out from under weight of
mass collapse (in long line of extinctions
since hydrogen depletion first
precipitated
              photosynthesis)
out into
         empty
              frontier space,
                              mammals

now nervously twitch whiskers—angle
ears, sniff every whiff of smoke-soaked air—
nibbling last scratch of seed or
dissipating flesh, black ink drop eyes
(small globes) alert
                    to everything.

Existence gathered in
                              Ten
million years, each day fresh horizons
dawn, far sun   65 MYA - *Paleogene*
              enticing ever further   *proliferation of*
up from burrowing oblivion   *mammals*
deep vision
              meeting wide expanse of light
now breaking over open planet.
Each day paints
              within thin eggshell skull

new furrows of experience
swelling in time to new capacities
to see & process earth's round promise
now unbound. Till breaking free (like sun
from the horizon)
                        ascendant brain
starts slowly to collect far-strewn
existence—gathering
                        to consciousness
this second earth compact of all
it sees & needs & can create, what is
and what might be—reflecting too
its deep and ambient lineage,
born into embrace
                        of change, planet
of possibility.

Modeling the world

                        Again new
energy revs up, explodes across
untethered continents, internalized
combustion purring to warm-blooded
touch, fine-tuning temperature to best
performance—high-test
                        grain distillate
cogenerating steady heat,
supercharging
                        brain to uptake
granulated earth. So in irruptive
millions, round-eyed, emerge from under-
ground, soft bundles of tight nerves, small
hands intent to wash smooth slate-gray
fur (incessantly
                        in heat or hope
of mate) or scamper back to darkness
at first hiss of remnant reptile
sidling through grass. Black *fledermäuse*
take to air, hypothesizing its
each angle, modeling

the world
in sound. While under lapis
                         oceans
go rollercoasting behemoth
cetaceans
            likewise each
                      sonically
in touch with one & all, half way round
whole sounding planet. Or up from
sentient seas—
                      spinner porpoises aloft
like fireworks, splash
                      down unfathomable
array of aqua sparks. Or flashing
gold across wind-driven plains, thunder
dark herds (sharp-hoofed & horned) as clouds
almost—close-scudding, leaping fleet, airborne—
in flight from
                following low tawny
carnivores.

Rich emerald matrix

            While all the while up tree
trunks like dark tunnels into deep green
solace climb (frog & rodent-like) small
primates, curious
                to squirrel out every   60 MYA – *early*
limb   *primates*
            in search of touch & taste of
                                        ripest
fruit—or fly among them synapse-like
to piece & puzzle whole
                      complexity
of forest (sea-like
                shimmering green
net of light) together into self-
same growing
                consciousness, body &
soul imprinted

as from womb with this
rich emerald matrix. Limbs
lengthening
to reach far limbs, hands radiating
out dendritic
spread to grasp high vining
lines, crisscrossing options where next to
connect, eyes
shifting forward to two-
angled focus modeling dense
volumetric space & distances
to judge unerringly exact what
point to target to hold onto, then
what point
release, all free & easy
(second natured)—so
your ancestry
rocks & rollicks springingly through freely
giving trees.

Digital manipulation

Periodic climate
shifts erase then re-establish
landscapes, dry to wet, grasses to forest,
back again
along great land-mass-birthing
rift of Africa. From which rhythmic
fecundity (earth breathing
in & out
rain forests, billowing, contracting
to bring forth
rich speciation as
far nebula does stars) one ape
descends
from islanded copses down
to ground to push out over open
grass seas
surging possibilities
and threat. Soon walking upright, tree-like,

5 MYA -
hominids

running with rippling wind—hard breathing
taking wind within (encompassing
savannah's sweep) hard beat

4.5 MYA - *hominid bipedalism*

        of heart then
drumming each wide stride across resounding
land, expanding, deepening, wide reach
of fingers, eyes & feet—dark clumps of
hominids maneuver into place
still gripping
        maybe sticks for balance
or to raise up ruckus, but
        hands free
now to pursue all manner of new
digital manipulation
for which
        forest had equipped us.

        He

toys stick into fire, rearranging
logs to structure
        calculated to
take in new air, repeatedly probes
embers fountaining sparks all directions.

To nest in hand caressingly

Now under open sky imagine
fitting hand to stone (perhaps picked up
along dry riverbed you're following—

2.3 MYA - *stone tools*

round geode, sharp obsidian washed
down volcanic slope) perhaps
        to crush
sweet marrow out from bone; then sharpening
in time to cut flesh off from carcass;
then from
        whole herd to separate stray
individual (gesturing in
concert with whole tribe which way to run,
stop, feint, cut back, then finally let

go barrage connecting over
distance, point to

point)—and in that process
flaking off also sharp sparks to nest

0.8 MYA - *fire*   eventually
domesticated
in grasses cupped in
hand to breathe caressingly into
bright flame at your command.

He raises

smoking stick to point.

Those embers
answered to the stars: Andromeda,
that speck 2.3 million light years
off (our nearest neighbor galaxy) first
chipped from its

conglomerate suns that light
that strikes your retina

tonight back when
first people chipped first tools.

Everything then known

Breathe life
into those embers, coaxing them to
fires warm as this encircling
this planet—our own faint galaxies
reflecting back far skies, each flickering
face reflecting, too, round

wonder.

Round
such circles, slowly, sounds & gestures—quick
glances, longish stares, premeditated
posturings—evolve, in concert with
enlarging brain (sustained by heart's sure
firing) ever

more fine-grained
communication. As if hard stone, found
sounds get chipped, shaped, sharpened into words

162

to track & represent things other
than themselves. One thing transforms then to
another (as predator
                              transfigures
flesh of prey—or statue turns lion's stare
on you), all reality subject
to be
              cut up, reconstituted
into human
                    ken, body & soul,
now separate from, now replicating whole.
Picture
              bright flash of recognition
passed round eye to eye as group arrives
at its conclusions, knowing among
themselves what's what, what's not, what might be
yet to come—so words get threaded, one
by one (like beads
                              elaborating
clothing warming one beyond bright weave
of fire) stitched together in long twining
stories faithfully repeating
everything then known to everyone
in patterns all agree on—
                              beautiful
as snakeskin helixing round limb, yet
modulating, too, occasionally
flame-like
              to new spark of insight fit
to survive abiding scrutiny.

To mind the earth

Or picture, once removed from sharp-eyed
fires, people merging two by two back
into night—removing (clasp by gasp, bone
buttons letting
                    loose) long flow of clothes
down onto ground—warm bodies following

to undulate as river moves
through hills, its ripples generating
new topographies, fresh heights, repeated
apogees—till in
            long time our bodies
sculpt themselves (as firm hand-fingered
earthen beads flow down her breast, his
rosary to crescent goddess) the shape
of earth, perfecting flesh to fit
& replicate
            earth's plenteous embrace.

So brain now closes round evolving
language, every word hard pearl sheened bright
as moon within dark churning musculature
of night—till stepping into morning
light, our own lithe species,

200,000 YA -
Homo sapiens
                        spears stone-tipped,
minds likewise tactical with ever
sharpening intent,
                        strikes out from

50,000 YA -
human diaspora
Africa across all continents
encompassing in its long strides, wide
eyes, far-reaching intellect, entire
scope of planet—emerald, gold & azure—
coalesced as knowledge
                        malleable
to make
            first sense and use of this
wide-spreading garden, and in the end
learn
            wondrously to mind the earth.

Seed and dance

Then taking that round comprehension
down (seed-like) into ground—as in deep
dream—we penetrate circuitous
down-rooting caverns snaking into

stone, there
           carve & paint impressions, bringing
forth smooth-contoured bounding antelope
and mammoth from
              dark swell of rock
now animate to touch of lightning
torch—then bounding up ourselves from planet's
depths to rounded ridge out front—tribe steps
out under dome of all shared consciousness;
points sticks; ignites
             bright fire flaring back
night sky; connects stars circling fierce
lion, bear, bull, white
             swan & ibex
dancing
         with them round wide universe
(one song lifting
           every creature up)
exchanging with them strengths
              to stir new birth.

*20,000 YA -
Magdalenian cave
paintings*

And spark as well, from such ancestral
tunnelings, those embryonic dreams
of all life lines inlaid within our own
development—all species there in
kinship one with us
           emergently
to have & hold, in mutual respect,
to husband caringly—and in shared
sacred trust, midwife
           prolific earth.

As when with flash of blade Odysseus
makes peace with goddess
           Circe to return
his men from animal to human
form, then at her invitation yields
hard intellect—boar-tested, tusk-scarred
at his thigh—into her yearning

chambers, the two compacting

                           mysteries

yet to be grasped.

           As in meiosis

parent genes first separate then turn

recombinant (harboring therein

best chance of newborn form), our species

now in ritual dance of consciousness

with earth spins

                wildly out of line, then

back in passionate embrace—mind

distancing

            to comprehend, then

comprehending self and universe

the same.

Hard genesis

           But memories, too, embedded

in old stories there recur—

               stirred back

perhaps by taste of salt entrained in rock

released again to flow through fluid

flesh hungering

            return to its wet

source—or peppering of carbon burnt

& flecked by fire's tongue (metabolic

process skewered, extroverted, turned

domestic) mouthwatering as flesh

again meets

         meaty flesh.

              Smoke trailing

my each move tonight, steeping hair,

blinding sight—black dragon

            conjured up

from half-tamed flame, following where mind

haphazardly

       now roams.

Back deep from first
hard push of species into consciousness,
hard genesis (like shells galactically
aswirl in limestone walls)—white smoke
uncoils ghost-like, chillingly, ghost
stories of
                    extinction hovering
above
          fires pressed down hard by wind off
ocean. More winds pushing
                              dunes from inland,
push as well to westernmost thin edge
of continent sparse bands of thinning
men & women, honed at extremities
of sifting climate. Driven there   70,000 YA – *human*
omnivorously they eke   *genetic constriction*
                         from every
crevice shellfish, mollusks, algae,
tooling
          diet to consume all things
and with it, mind to pick apart all
surfaces, extract new energies
to underwrite refreshed conglomerate
expansiveness—releasing growing
time to gestate, age
                      and contemplate;
to play, create; to procreate
intense
          attention—as to a child or
mate or anything that feeds or threatens
them. Adapting finally not ourselves
but earth at large to fit inbred
conceptions of it, bloodily we track
behind us
                everywhere we step
                                    wide
footprints of extinction ever haunting
us—fear forever at our backs.

Soon overflowing from cupped hands

Fire metaphoric boils off.
Fire metabolic (taken in, then
out again in hand) we carry
with us, prized possession, rendering
'the ends of earth' our own, Promethean
digesting it.

Still toying with stout sticks
brought down from forest, people probe flush
riverbanks in search
of roots, at first

13,000 YA - *latest*
Pleistocene
glaciers retreat

unconsciously, then noticing
disturbance generating flourishes
of grain—which taken up in hand and
scattered (first perhaps on threshing wind)
inseminates again
fresh furrowed
earth, releasing her abundance to
fresh touch
of minds increasingly adept.

12,600 YA –
agriculture,
settlements

Soon overflowing from cupped hands, grain
floods, supple & undulant
as lovers
following long separation—flowing,
filling, over & again, round pots
hand-fashioned from wet clay, smoothed, fired hard,
spiral-incised—eventually from
granaries
at core of villages,
then cities, quickly overflowing—
people
able now to grow, hold, store,
trade sustenance out-spiraling all
earlier capacity of earth—
new universe

initialized, sketched out
in dirt, rotund as cornucopia.

Wind turns on us, fire hissingly split-
tongued escaping out beyond

stone ring.

Blades glistening

To touch and taste rich harvest—green blade
unfurled from perfectly placed seed, red
droplet tongued from clustered grape held
up (finger to thumb) to blush of light
to judge

how sweet & potent vintage
might become—wise eyes first trace

wide circling

sky through years and generations (stand
stones to calendar imprint of heaven
onto yielding earth); learn

guidance of
hand, foot & hoe in ripening
alignment with round coursing seasons; then
gather up gold grains innumerable
as stars—pomegranates drooping amber
full, red apple flecked with fingerprints
of light. Accounting

cyclic annual
surplus, warlords locust-like wheel in
from plains down sweeping metal scythes through
populace long laboring (as from
slow motion nightmare) to outrun
red flood now running down

blades glistening
coldly as crescent moon.

Soon

full

grown

symbiosis—systemic violence—
plants fear, reaps subservience within
each person, then at plundered heart
of every village, pumps up ruler
once himself
                    marauder (hunkered down
now round ripe cellars) insistent only
to increase production flooding out
to feed insatiable cohort of kin—
as coils of old serpent tightening
at depth of spine
                         each breath you take makes
harder to unwind. Or as new-minted
ancient mitochondria
                              once set
up shop inside host cells to guard rich store
of chlorophyll from unintended
consequence of surplus oxygen
set free by its own industry. Or as
red fire ant
                    adds bite at base of thorn
defending sweet acacia as its
own.

*5,500 YA - rulers,
organized warfare,
cities, writing*

Lines cut

          Hard words, hard lines, cut cuneiform
in mud, then cooked,
                         record, count out,
apportioning abundance—then set
forth anticipation
                    of next month,
create demand beyond
                         what cut
of flesh alone could yield.
                              Sharp words, sharp
blades accordingly direct eyes down—
to cut with metal plows
                         soft earth, to
cut canals to moisten roots, cut roads

through fields (wheels bearing down heavy with
harvest), cut silver seas (sharp-keeled ships
heaving forward dark wine cargos, salt
furrows waked behind), cut
                              whiplash lines
across bare backs to bind and organize
whole enterprise.

Acropolis alive with glyphs
                    Then reaching up to skies
again, small sovereigns open further
lines communicating
                    high intents
direct from the divine, rerouting
long-lived earth and human ties to new
allegiances to latest order
from on high—thus binding opened wounds
of flesh and ground
                         with gauze of greater
purpose, stepping up, constructing grand
acropolis
              from which to govern
hearts. Sliced from hard dolomite & marble
(once bright precipitate of sea life
long compressed, now rising up again
ascending strata) mountain
                              pyramids
shine forth across bare sands and cloud-cloaked
forest—Giza to Yucatan
inspiring, alive with fresh-chipped
glyphs & pictographs—recording, yes,
last count of all
                    those slain & sacrificed
last ritual war, or all out fight, last
ball court game to gain high honor for
all out eternity—high desert
mausoleums (embalming toxins
jarred within) coldly
                    certifying

5,000 YA - *state
religions*

171

everlasting rule and ruler. One
by one, stones cut, dragged, grappled up &
into place now grapple with hard fact
of death now grown foundational,
ascendant—death

                           pressed into service,
drafted and abstracted into war,
death
               institutionalized to serve
all institutions, unifying
all in ultimate
               division of
all earth carved up, served up to human
purpose, divinity
            itself
domesticated, herded off to
slaughter on stone altar. Blood spills
                       down
steps to fill
            each letter of each law
incised in stone, illumined and
alive as neon.

To know firsthand

            Nearby, relaxing
along riverbank, ensconced in soft
meanders, laborers (observant
of first labor law, sweet Sabbath, ode
to peace at heart of creativity)
raise up full cups, write down

                    soft song—words
flowing out through watery touch of brush
to textured
           parchment meshed from reeds still
swaying music of merged wind & current,
gravity, all
          pulling at their roots
invoking countless whisperings—all
longing back to true mountain springs, shared

sources—or forward also longing
towards upwelling
                        of new unities
within all people, all creation.
Some wander off in couples then, some
in small groups (wherever two or more
of you), some back to caves in mountain
wilderness
                to know firsthand the Oneness
understood to be
                        divine. As we
lounge here this night around warm fire, its
pine incense permeating air &
us & all of this that we breathe in
and out again as one—as music
drifting from
                        expert lips on woodwind
crafted in love's long pursuit, fluted
inspiration of
                all stories ever
told. Among them, in conclusion,
bone-tired Odysseus emerges
from last cave & pounding surf—washed up, all
epic talk and artifice of war
washed out, left far
                        afield—returning
now to fertile land and love, lost home
from which his future life might yet
in peace evolve.

2,700 YA – *Homer,
'The Odyssey'*

Be rich

                        The fire only embers
now suffuses us.

                        So everyone
take out one dollar. Tomorrow you
may need this. But recognize up here
how useless it's become. If nothing
else, take that awareness home. Be rich

with what you've learned.
                              Examine closely, see
every day you carry paper
pyramid
                    like young republic it
now represents (full faith & credit)
earthly evolving governance we each
breathe life into—tender hard won, always
undone. Founded in stone, its apex
hovers
              in blinding light, one eye
of ever widening awareness
taking in &
                        shining out—round globe
of iterative perception—earth become
energized and radiant as sun.
So let us pledge ourselves our sacred
words here on
                        this altar mountaintop
to burn each in deep passion to redeem
our lives compact in commonwealth
with all earth's life. In witness of, this
currency I now ignite and offer
up, its signature
                        inscribed on air.

1775 -
*American
Revolution*

Embrace of universe

Now build in mind firm courses towards new
noosphere—rondure
                        of knowledge ringing
planet comprehensively—science
integrated & attuned as music
of all spheres once whispered one shared
language. The building of the tower
thus resumes:
                    Copernicus, Kepler
and Galileo, then Newton, lay
out far continuity of space

1543 -
*Copernicus,
'On the
Revolutions of
Celestial
Spheres'*

1609 - *Kepler,
'The New
Astronomy'*

1610 - *Galileo,
'Starry
Messenger'*

(to p.187)

Jose's Eulogy
(I look for him)

I look for him in tree leaves, breathing
with each breath of breeze. The atmosphere
is his, the hills that hold us in
embrace. I sense him everywhere, my
breath and body also his, each word
I speak passed down and risen up from
him, as tree trunk holds & spreads new leaf
each spring, eventually releasing
all to air and earth to dance free over
autumn graves. So he lives on in all
in us, deep root down reaching through
the earth to hold and touch whole forest
breathing with what love he grew and left.

Lily's Song
(river stone)

I found this river stone
so smooth & huge I thought
it must be egg of some long gone
unhatched *Velociraptor*
but way bigger & much smarter
heading towards us.
      I touched
the top of it, like nosecone rising
up from stream.
      Then thought
how polished, as if water
over years imparted its
own surface onto rock —
as child might mirror parent yet
all the same be different.

May be there's hope that way.
Some things should go extinct.

Then thinking: stone could be
round belly
everyone would want to touch
like font at front of church.

Cleanse & protect us, each repeats.
Be blessed in this new birth.

Reeding, Riting, Rhyth-matic
(Meru)

Reeding

I reed all day whenever
possible — (*down by thee
riverside, down by your
riverside*) — I curl all syllables
to shape of you, to shape
of me, to swirl of river's
music, musing cosmically.
We eddy, you & me, I reed
you circling me, we sway
to pull of earth, to stir of star,
to swivel hip to hip all day.

Riting

Best times I rite — mornings
mostly, but could be
any time & place I see
sky opening to earth, earth
rush to sea, or fire everywhere.
I rite the world consuming me.
I rite us all together here.
I rite each particle of dust
incarnate and transfiguring
all things. I drink the air, taste
music there, commute
death sentences to life
set free, commune intoxicant
brief sung to all creation.

Rhyth-matic

Imagine
stillness

as you spin
1,000
miles an hour
round
earth lapping
then
round sun
1.6 million
miles a day
& then
again

long arm of galaxy gesturing you into
its spiral
sweep

itself
as well
revolving locally
elliptically
in

dance with
sister galaxies red-shifting out
from one imagined
cosmic

center
we are said to be
at center
of
:

each breath
be still
with
this

.

Gwen's Practice

Frog Pose

You feel it—
thighs nested into calves & chest,
feet flat catapults,
arms outstretched anticipating
action—
mostly in your eyes.

Hawk Pose

Arms wide as wings
for hours silently you sing
nothing but
you and air—and then

the whole sky breathing.

Serpent Pose

Flat out on earth
some day I am the way
the universe
                gives way
releasing everything
stars even
                out

to drift to this
snowballing planet
to ignite

                quick-flickering
tongue, round-spiraled
belly
        down to earth
& basking in
                warm sun.

Marta's Prayer
(O)

O
I am
(!)
of
the

round
earth
round
universe

expanding
known
horizons
what
could
be

forever
always
infinitely
—
yet

also
death

re-gathers
&
rebirths

contracting
fertile
mix

so
long
so

mystery
goes
on

.

Group Popcorn Poem
(what if)

What if:
Our highways fueled themselves from wildflowers
& grasses grown in medians?

What if:
We earmarked earth's inheritance of fossil energy
solely to jump-start clean renewables?

What if:
My wordcheck didn't flag as incorrect "renewables"
or "sustainably"?

What if:
The only wars were fought in history books?

What if:
The wealth milked from five centuries & six continents
was spent to heal the damage done
to earth and us?

What if:
Instead of resource, forests were deep-rooted
birthright of the earth?

What if:
The rights of plankton to secure their place under the sun
took precedence to plastic
gyred oceans?

What if:
We understood plankton breathe out
for us more oxygen, take in more carbon from our burnings
than even forests?

What if:
The ocean had a voice and forests spoke?

What if:
They had the vote—
proportionate in global governance to populations
of all species under peaceful sway
of wave and canopy?

What if:
We learn to speak
their way?

Vince's Song
(I stand)

I stand
for all that would have been
(and could be, dream-time traveling)
if we knew then
what we do now.

I stand
for Adirondack watershed
trees towering to climax
over & again forever able to sustain
their kind in equilibrium
with mine, who walk soft-footed
under reach of up-stretched wide protectorate
of sky, protecting it, each leaf,
to net the rain, wash down
particulates to earth again, breathe in
black carbon simmering
sunlight to green
lucidity, then underfoot, to rest awhile, release
pure flow downstream into steeled
city of skywalking dreams.

I stand
for Seminoles still poling black
backwaters giving back green/yellow flash
of parakeet & thunder clap of 'Lord God' bird
still drumming at
ghost cypress.

I stand
for Mississippian flood plains
bank full, ten million mother-of-pearl
dawn pigeons passing, flood gates
replaced with our sure wisdom
flood will come—will build
back continent, wide-welcoming all riches
earth deposits, keeping free & open all her
currencies to carve land fluid and

resilient as great river going
its own way, our own concerted songs
carried along.

I stand
for the Dakotas rolling out deep
harmonies of grass sequestering
each strain of wind down into reed & grain
& root of plain, one interwoven basket brimming
bison like dark herds of cumulus adrift
across this land, unfenced.

I stand
with Navajo who hold the sacred
mountains, who weave sunrise
to turquoise skies (each day unique
as fingerprint of dawn), who radio
intelligence indecipherable to those
not native here, like magpies
wise to harm.

I stand
for Inuit, salmon & orca totem
people, guardians of oceans, ice cap
keepers, sending out from mouth of every
circumpolar stream & river emissaries
to unite and dance all nations to one
song of our return to common home
to nest and nuzzle earth
to flesh, release self back
downstream to pure
dark depths.

I stand
with ochre pipestone, black obsidian
flaked off trade rock once
returning over high Sierra pass, seeding
like starlight still this future
I now travel. Let us return wide westward
valley to wild rice, wild snow geese
blizzarding
riparian reservoirs brimful for granite

cities, accumulating fields, unsilted bay—then let
us raise, first, mountain havoc cry
up to disintegrating sky, then widening dome
of care to shelter here white winter
water pooled each year,
intricate as finch's song, quiet as its
feathers oaring air.

Mo's Song
(ethics of predation)

Know what you
consume.

Make pacts
with it.

Consider
consequence.

Be skillful
not to cause

pain. Play a lot
in practice. Practice

in the kill
restraint,

patience
in the wait,

gratitude
in everything.

Hunt wisdom
and fall prey

to mystery.

June's Creation Song
(God's asking)

God's asking in the garden,
"Where are you?"
Don't answer over-trippingly.
God knows. Allow her
steps to resonate. Allow
yourself the space to set
aside doubt's comfortable
attire. Stand there bare
as you were born, but now aware
divinity is what you meet within
and learn to grow. God's in
the garden flowering with all
you do and feel and know.

like clockwork—moons, suns & planets dancing
elliptically in unison. Then
Lyell projects
                    same continuity
through time to move stones glacially, then all
geology. Then
                    Darwin, picking
up the pulse, connects all life, arrayed
from islanded finches to entangled
bank—one fabric weaving of itself
selectively
                    infinities
of novelty to meet sifting demands
of time and space and life's own changing
inclinations.
                    Inclining steeply,
Einstein, Heisenberg and Hubble
blow out hard boundaries of thought, show
matter at its core translates to
energy, all being equal, yet
in infinite
                    expansion bubbling
each instant new creation—unity
& innovation, atom &
galaxy, in constant flux, each
influencing the rest. Then Higgs, et.
al., excite
                    half century of search
to fish out source of mass itself
from vacancy of universe. From which
as well, Watson & Crick
                              decant one
spiral molecule (deoxyribo-
nucleic acid) intent on harvest
of rich randomness in order
to survive & then spin forth, whole cloth, long
bolt of living cosmos.
                    To bring back

1687 - *Newton,
'Mathematical
Principles of
Natural
Philosophy'*

1830 - *Lyell,
'Principals of
Geology'*

1859 - *Darwin,
'On the Origin
of Species'*

1905 - *Einstein,
'On the Electro-
dynamics of
Moving Bodies'*

1927 -
*Heisenberg,
'uncertainty
principle'*

1929 - *Hubble,
'A Relation
between
Distance and
Radial Velocity
among Extra-
galactic Nebula'*

1964 - *Higgs,
'Broken
Symmetries and
the Masses of
Gauge Bosons'*

2012 - *Large
Hadron
collider detects
Higgs Boson*

1953 - *Watson &
Crick, 'Molecular
Structure of
Nucleic Acids'*

home Lovelock & Margulis strike up same
strands, same strains

from molecule to cell
to planet, single oceanic
symphony

of life, rock, water, air
and energy—now self-conducting,
self-aware, in growing consciousness
evolving, and therefore responsible
to what

this polished, ever-rounding
globe becomes. Bent on as Carson warned
silenced unraveling. Or rising

up and passing on hard-won baton
as Goodall gesturing

in still forest
reaches out—mind meeting

mind—to touch
deep chords connecting us within
embrace of universe.

Round planet caged

Heads spinning,
such expansiveness spreads out as well
across material planet,
modern diaspora

from Europe
everywhere. Pragmatic Bacon
extracts from wondrous alchemy new

science bound in servitude to dim
gold-glimmering horizons. Descartes
cuts off

thought from existence, netting
all reality in mesh of
mathematical

belief—men free
to cut all things and beings up to what
design best suits best minds. It gets us
to the moon in time, but first divides

oceans & earth (lined longitude and
latitude tied up
         to sky) directing
exploration of all corners of
round planet, caged—like bear, fattened from birth,
immobilized, flesh gridded raw
into steel bars the better to extract
some bile some
         cut-off human thinks
an aphrodisiac. Or facing
into western wind—skin lined & chiseled
raw to chart new course to gain gold sun—
inspired captains calculate their rich
returns, triangulating
         cold
Atlantic, human sinews lashed
below for rum for Yankee cash. Fast
ships tacking over tortuous
abyss transfer raw muscle cubicled
to lay base base
         of cotton-fibered
pyramids, world economic engine
tuned steel-shackle tight.

Homo carboniferous

         Then driving steel
cross continent, men dynamite black
anthracite to crack, pick, transport,
burn
       industrial respiring
to sizzle wired net synapsing
commerce; mainline
         deep pitch distillate
of life; needle down steel spikes through giving
earth to spasm carboniferous
rush
       of energies banked temperately
all living history (income of sun
rebalanced to pass down inheritance

*1865 - Industrial
Revolution, slaves
freed, oil harnessed*

of planet prospering within
life's means). Gone up in smoke, black gusher
carbon
     streams & canopies treelike
through air—swamp forest risen from dark
vault, brief shimmering illusory
last gasp, last splash exuberance, snake-oil

1945 – *A-bomb announces Anthropocene era of planetary human impact*

wavering off superheated desert.
Dragon
     hallucination (as mushroom
cloud exploding
       growth) now towering

1985 – *human population exceeds 5 billion. 6th mass extinction of species accelerates*

above all else, flares off combustion
breath, unfurls wide wings—scaled iridescent
neon green, gold, red—to caramelize
high skies—whole biosphere tied tight, white
con trails ribboning

1988 - *NASA testifies to Congress on climate crisis*

     high heavens, highest
Hope
    dissipating to exhaust
of antiquated lizards blowing
smoke. This world now

1992 - *United Nations earth summit & climate treaty*

       return to and resolve,
yours going forward to decide. This
storm-bellied black-cloud dragon poke

2009 - *Copenhagen climate summit collapses*

back to subservience. This story has
no other end or hero—but to
do so, tame too your own
       blast-fevered,
black-consumpted pride to burn instead
inside with measured warmth, with tempered
heart, with practiced, rhythmic self-restraint—
in deep humility to place hands on
whole earth
     to see her through
       defining
hot contractive crisis.

Go forth and sing

You can expand
out thought and feeling far as human eye
and all technology can see, head
circling accumulating new
infinities intoxicating
now in view

> but must, at last, come back

to this one planet

to apply long

healing touch and celebratory
nurture—so to grow in unison
and grace deeply through time. So stand here now
at furthest reach of this resilient
Eden, high pitch

of oceanic sphere,

zenith of summer sun, expectant
of your own new birth, and gather in
your strength each breath—here

islanded from

surrounding flood, at rest on wildness
still

emergent—simply to see, eyes

open as wide earth and universe
(and blinking back old tears, new fears) not
overburdened but set free

by mountain

to descend now into surging sea
of ever endless possibility,
armed not

so much with knowledge as

intent—to know the whole as much as you
can learn, and act as best you can
in consciousness of that—know mind & heart
& body, all of it connecting
with all else.

Beyond particulars,
beyond cyclic hypothesis, there is

*1903 – human flight
at Kitty Hawk*

*1968 - Apollo moon
shot photographs
'Earthrise'*

this sense
　　　　of everything—
　　　　　　　　　　one long
abiding and aspiring song.

Feel stir within
　　　　　　of God evolving,
wholeness taking hold
　　　　　　　　　each breath—as quiet
hymn
　　　strengthens & steadies flame within.
So mostly now go forth and sing.

9

. . .

. . .

. . .

Day Nine

Return

Long exhale coming down off mountain,
trail switchbacking, mind repetitive
& turning
            in on self. This morning
ashen to my eyes as that last touch
to test cold fire ring. Then
                        slowly gold
sun burns its way down through to us
again, and spirits rise to meet new day—
conversing as young
                jumbled rocks ring
back our words downsplashing hollowly
through canyon.

                As in deep dreamtime world
we lay hands on metallic car—sleek
natural creature basking in fresh sun—
appreciating everything
compressed
                therein (mined & manufactured
from broad earth) then burnished down to this
identity
        like warbler singing its
unique, mysterious expression
up from dust of our
                long trail. (These notes

now coming to an end.) And everyone
here glad to rest tired
                    feet, change into
something fresh, let metal hurtle us
back toward familiar cushions and
constraints.

                    Long talk drive down Pacific
slope. I'm at the wheel, Mo riding
shotgun. Regenerative each time we
brake, the car downloads pent energy
of earth: we're slaloming whole mountain
riding wave of gravity down crest
pushed up from ocean, breaking now back
west. Each touch of fingertip translates
intentions—roundnesses caressed down
column angling into alignment
& smooth granulated flow of road
out-spiraling before us: all one
weaving of connection spun from long
movement on and on forever seeming
this one moment ours.
                    'Riverrine
bacteria,' Mo's postulating,
'first precipitated metals out
from streams (that bear high mountains in
suspension) veining earth with ore—thank them
for this.'
          'Thank plankton,' I say, 'snowing
sunlight down into black depths compressed
to fuel continuance.'
                    So words drift
down, go sideways, piling up. Any
of any value here,
                    not mine to tell.

Pit stop. Losing elevation. Sweet
pine ejaculate fills air here, cakes
cars gold. I'm heady with intoxicant

of scent, memories returning, pitch
taste of first
                    retsina, one warm-fire
evening, bottle pulled from snow like cork
from bottle opening to warm us
from within—
                    here, now, new pine sap rising
up entire ponderosa into
air, releasing same elixir—as
warm tar
                    on open road or prow
of jet black ship pushed up from wine-fresh
sea to rest a moment motionless
in sand's caress.
                    I drink it in, then
back on roll, air thickening as we
descend. Sharp smoke from forest burn, bark
beetles having breached defenses stressed
by fevered winds off fields & cities
piling into mountains.
                    Then flat out
stew of dust & pesticides stirred thick
and left to stand in basin peppered with
petroleum nutrients, growing
(mushrooms from spore) development
blacktopping yielding depths of country's
productivity.
                    Hit wall of stench,
cow city, methane percolating
skyward.
                    Roads then in confluence, cars
weaving torrents down through coast range, trucks
dieseling delivery of valley
cubed & crated up for sale, concrete
constricting into city. Air here
itself fine aggregate, particulate
conglomerate. One hardly breathes, mind
being boxed. Hands holding tight to wheel,
one comes to this: 'So easily it ends.'

So now, alone, again. On board and
waiting. Put on once more

                           soft amber
Lepidopteran Mom gave me, jeweled
droplet at my breast, rounding into
it far reach of life—back some warm sunny
day, sweet carboniferous sap so
flowed that life then took its fill and still
here offers back to me.

                        Like that, this
mountain wildness I shall hold & carry
in me all this life—as also
ocean laps within each cell, or flame
flicks off from atom forged within first
burst of universe, first fire of
creation: that roundly I declare
I'll carry

                  and pass on—and on, round
earth encircling, electron-like,
to light long spiraling passages
ahead.

          Jet wheels into alignment,
lights writing large the way

                     the infinite
forever vanishes. Throttle down
runway, off up into the smoothing
air, head back to take all in. Off left
the city lifts

                white mountain, lights just
coming on, each window its own
individual world, while westward, sun
slants down last strokes off every flick
& fleck of wave & each cell of each leaf
dances to day's final touch, earth turning
east. And with it plane

                 banks, steadies
into climb. And into me, leaned back

I'm thinking
          furrowing moist futures
now to round to—how ecology
of carboniferous could teach us
to rebalance
          measured air. (One reason
to write Mo, I'm thinking. Now on
this stone planet ours

          to bear.) Below
soft light suffusing whole hot valley
every field seems
          tinted, cut to fit
huge stained glass window—as if the earth
this moment were to be
          crafted to
cathedral, what mysteries in it
to see & celebrate & carry on
we're only guessing at.

          Now darkening,
small towns tucked streamside among foothills
one by one become
          first embers, then
small galaxies adrift on deepening
immensity.

          Then rising fast, eyes front
again, high mountain offers up to sky
wide spreading
          emptiness, rich as
deep earth—steep slate of night on which
caringly to write
          our star-sown dreams.

Storyline of Cosmic Evolution

Time	Event	Page
13.7 BYA	'Big bang' creates time & space.	*53*
13.6996 BYA	Hydrogen, helium and lithium atoms form.	*56*
13.3 BYA	Stars form from hydrogen.	*10, 61*
13.2 BYA	Stars & supernovae start forming heavier elements.	*11*
12.0 BYA	Oldest detected water molecules.	*24*
4.56 BYA	Sun forms.	*12*
4.54 BYA	Earth forms.	*12*
4.53 BYA	Moon forms.	*14*
4.3 BYA	Crust hardens, rains come.	*27*
4.3 BYA	Oceans form.	*30*
4.0 BYA	Life forms on earth.	*36*
3.9 BYA	Life here invents photosynthesis	*37*
3.0 BYA	Moon freezes. Last lunar volcanoes.	*14*
2.9 BYA	Oxygen crisis builds.	*73*
2.5 BYA	Ozone layer forms.	*75*
2.4 BYA	Aerobic respiration evolves.	*79, 98*
2.0 BYA	Eukaryotic cells evolve.	*101*
1.2 BYA	Multicellular organisms evolve.	*110*
1.0 BYA	Heterotrophy arises.	*103*
1.0 BYA	Sexual reproduction arises.	*107*

Storyline of June's Week

Key to Characters and Songs

Acknowledgments and Sources

Evolutionary cosmologist Brian Thomas Swimme and the late theologian Thomas Berry pioneered much of the terrain covered by this poem in their foundational book, *The Universe Story*, which extrapolates the science of the last half century into a coherent and inspiring world view. Berry's *The Dream of the Earth* and Swimme's *The Universe is a Green Dragon*, among many other essays and videos, further extend and elaborate their explorations.

Swimme also collaborated with Mary Evelyn Tucker to create the film and book, *Journey of the Universe,* and worked with Sidney Liebes and Elisabet Sahtouris to publish an illustrated timeline of the cosmos, *A Walk Through Time.* Taking to heart Berry's charge to realign all human disciplines with this emergent 'Great Story,' Reverend Michael Dowd and his wife Connie Barlow have energetically spread the word among religious institutions, culminating in Dowd's *Thank God for Evolution!* And of course the seminal video poetry of Carl Sagan's *Cosmos* series opened the eyes of my generation to the wonder and awe embedded in the scientific revelations of our time.

Closer to home, the early drafts of the poem received keen and caring scrutiny from Mary Reynolds Thompson, author of *Reclaiming the Wild Soul.* Mark Livingston likewise painstakingly reviewed the final text. The book evolved to completion with the word by word attention and encouragement of fellow writers Bruce

Thompson, Terri Glass and Sam Ciofalo. Sam was also my back-packing partner of many summers, sharing Sierra scenes and insights that helped shape the poem. The comments and examples of many other friends and acquaintances have also contributed, often without them knowing so.

Finally, my exploration of the universe story, and life itself, has been an ever deepening mutual journey of discovery with my wife and soul mate, Tamra Peters. Together, we have traveled to distant shores, gloried in the natural wonders everywhere around us, conducted *Ecos* classes and excursions, raised our voices in support of eco-conscious governance, and reminded ourselves to savor each moment—all the while engaged in an on-going conversation with each other and the earth. That conversation and love richly inform these pages.

William Carney's poetry has been awarded two American Academy of Poets prizes and a Hutchinson Fellowship at Williams College. His previous books include *Cities*, a nuclear peace epic published in 1985. As a landscape architect, he oversaw the design and construction of Yerba Buena Gardens in San Francisco. He started telling the story of the universe as a camp naturalist in Cincinnati, Ohio, and a field biologist at Philmont National Scout Ranch in New Mexico. He now lives and writes in northern California, where he is active in the climate movement.

Made in the USA
San Bernardino, CA
20 March 2014